Design Concepts

A BASIC GUIDEBOOK

Gail Lynn Hartwigsen

MICHIGAN STATE UNIVERSITY

Allyn and Bacon, Inc.

BOSTON   LONDON   SYDNEY

Library of Congress Cataloging in Publication Data

Hartwigsen, Gail Lynn.
   Design concepts.

   Bibliography: p.
   Includes index.
   1. Design. 2. Interior decoration.
3. Architectural design. I. Title.
NK1510.H33   729   79-11983
ISBN 0-205-06663-1

Production Editor: Sandy Stanewick
Manufacturing Buyer: Linda Jackson

Printed in the United States of America

Design Concepts

A BASIC GUIDEBOOK

CONTENTS

PREFACE

Methodology involves the systematic breakdown of a body of knowledge into its workable parts. The knowledge is broken down because individual problems are easier to solve than those having multiple aspects. The individual parts are then assembled sequentially, according to the most desirable route through the subject.

The table of contents of this book represents its methodological sequence and, therefore, the route that the student will take while learning the basics of an interior design and housing curriculum. The book is meant to be read sequentially. The order of the topics may not always agree with you and there may be times when you will want to abandon the sequence temporarily, but I have arranged the book in what I have found to be the logical order for the accumulation of design and housing knowledge. Following it as closely as possible should produce the best results.

This book is not intended to be a single resource for an introductory interior design and housing course. Indeed, it *should* be supplemented, ideally with readings from the bibliography and possibly a source dealing with graphic or artistic details for drawing. Intregating these auxiliary sources with this book should provide a total classroom format. Nevertheless, I respect the originality of each course and leave the choice of accompanying readings, texts, and classroom activities entirely to the discretion of the instructors. Their selections will give the course its individual personality.

This book is not an exhaustive authority on all of the subjects it introduces. The key word here is "introduce." The intention of this publication is to do just that: *introduce* students to the aspects of design that are essential to the professional fields of interior design and housing. Students *can* effectively explore these subjects on an elementary level and, at the same time, gain experience upon which to draw for future use as professionals in major design projects and writings.

It has been said that the less people know about a subject, the more they are apt to learn about it. As they become more familiar with a subject, they become more selective about what they will pursue within that field. It is with that belief that I wrote this book—to expose beginning students to the broad aspects of a complex subject before they become too familiar with subjects of particular interest to them.

CHAPTER ONE

AWARENESS

Why are some parts of town successful and others unsuccessful? Why do people choose to live in one neighborhood instead of another? Why do children learn better in one environment than in another?

How aware of your surroundings are you? Do you find yourself taking note of small, seemingly insignificant details? Sometimes we go through the day in a fog and don't notice what is going on around us. We become so conditioned that it takes a great change in our environment to grab and maintain our attention.

The fields associated with interior design and housing deal with the physical environment and what goes on within it. The primary concern of these fields is to improve human life. People are the focal point: we scrutinize and analyze human behavior in an attempt to create better living, working, and playing conditions. Human behavior is subtle. So is the environment.

Starting today, *right now*, in fact, begin taking notice of everything. Notice people's expressions, attitudes, preferences. Watch for changes on the street where you live: When was that building torn down? When was that house repainted? How long has that store been there?

Watch everything. Question everything. Wonder about it all. Does it make sense or not? Become inquisitive. Return to the "why, why, why?" stage of life. Become a devil's advocate. Suggest change. Be *difficult* at times.

Remember what you notice and put it to use in your planning. Remember the positive along with the negative. As you go through this book and actually begin to design spaces, you should begin to realize the value of the information that you have collected. Sooner or later, you will use everything you know, so start packing it into your head right away.

You will have to work on raising your awareness level. Several exercises are provided for this purpose at the back of the book (see Worksheets 1 and 2).

UNIT ONE

DESIGN THEORY

OBJECTIVES

Upon completion of this unit, you should be able to:

1. Utilize several thought processes to improve your creativity.
2. Organize and solve a problem methodically.
3. Through application, identify human values as they influence designed spaces.
4. Utilize the theories of physical, social, and psychological space as they influence designed spaces.

Design involves a lot more than just choosing a particular place to put something because you happen to like it that way. Before you tackle any problem, you have to investigate its components as thoroughly as possible. This unit presents some basic design theory to help with your investigation.

The chapter on *creativity* illustrates some ways in which you can become more creative. The following chapters on *values* and *space* give you background in human behavior that is directly applicable to space planning. You really cannot design spaces for human use unless you are cognizant of people themselves. Then, a chapter on *methodology* gives you a format into which the preceding three chapters fit. Methodology describes the process in which you organize all of the information you gather throughout the investigation of your problem. The theoretical information in this unit will help in later chapters when you will actually design spaces for people.

CHAPTER TWO

CREATIVITY

OBJECTIVES

Upon completion of this chapter, you should be able to:

1. Utilize five design tools to increase your idea production.
2. Define ideation, idea quantity, and imagineering.
3. Through analysis, identify and solve a given problem creatively.

Creativity is a complicated subject. To begin with, it is mental and intangible. It is not something you can hold in your hand, but then again, you can often spot it in a crowd. It can linger, but has been known to escape without warning. Indeed, it can be present and not even noticed!

Creativity involves thinking, and that is what this chapter deals with, namely, cultivating your thought process. Getting you to realize that the "gift" of coming up with new ideas is not necessarily dependent upon chance. *You can do it* if you put your mind to it. It takes dedication. The techniques described in this chapter will enable you to find out more about your problem in a way that requires hardly moving from your seat. All five of them have a close relationship to the design fields.

What is creativity? Who is creative? Would you agree with these statements: "Some people are just naturally more creative than others"; "I wasn't born with a lot of creativity, so I can't be expected to think of as many unique ideas as some other people"?

Creativity probably is a debatable subject. Some people are undoubtedly more creative than others. Some people just seem to be able to come up with numerous original ideas and others look to them for guidance. Is it by accident that creativity seems to have been doled out unevenly, or could there be a method to it? Whatever the answer to this question, you will now discover that there are ways in which you can increase your idea production, which is the basis of creativity. Creativity, in short, is the process of coming up with new ideas.

Three words and phrases come to mind at this point, and all are essential to the development of your creative skills. *Ideation* refers to the mental process itself. To ideate means "to think," and that is, of course, what you are going to be training yourself to do: think in new and unique ways. Second, *idea quantity* means that the person who is capable of producing the largest number of ideas per unit of time has the greatest chance of producing a truly significant one. In other words, the odds of your coming up with a really creative idea are best if you have a lot of ideas from which to select. Third, the word that probably describes best what we are doing here is *imagineering*, letting your imagination soar and then engineering it back to reality. Be careful to proceed in that order. In other words, don't confine yourself to reality and all of its constraints before you begin thinking of ideas. Think outlandishly, originally, and recklessly at first. You will not use all of your strange ideas; you only have to choose one good one. Most important, the longer you spend thinking of ideas, the more apt you are to produce a really wild one. After all, many great technological advances have been made because someone was not afraid to think differently and speak of unique ideas.

Why do you want to think of so many great ideas? Because design involves problem solving and problem solving demands idea production.

There seems to be a mental set, or state of mind, that is associated with creativity. Think of yourself in your most creative moments. Certain conditions and attitudes are usually present. The first one that comes to mind is a positive attitude. Don't dismiss your own or another's ideas too quickly. Articulate them, listen to them fully, and then, if possible, piggyback (add) other ideas to them. Talking through ideas with another person or a group can help in their development. An example is *brainstorming*, a group process in which several people, for a given amount of time, gather together and discuss a particular problem. During this time, they all contribute *positive* thoughts to the discussion and try to produce a workable solution. Allowing an idea to evolve beyond its initial inception and having patience throughout the process may prove to be a very worthwhile decision on your part. *Keep an open mind!*

Something just mentioned in passing really deserves much more attention. The practice of *patience* cannot be overemphasized. Don't be too anxious to come up with the perfect solution: your well-aimed arrow may end up hitting the wrong target. Think of it this way: instead of charging after that last quarter you dropped as you desperately tried to get a soda out of the machine, wait a minute, watch where it stops, then calmly go over and pick it up. It will do wonders for your composure, not to mention others' impression of your coolness under pressure. The point is this: hear an idea out fully before issuing any edicts about what will be and what won't be. Patience utilized in this manner may save you some otherwise wasted worry and energy. Try it.

The next prerequisite to creativity is faith and confidence in yourself. Say what you feel. Question what you do not understand. Speak out when you disagree with something. Let your thoughts be known: maybe someone else will hear them and will help you to develop them into a successful venture. Don't be afraid to have some criticism thrown at you. Constructive criticism can be very helpful and you should seek it. Don't be afraid to try something new. If you seem to be struggling with a concept or an object, throw it out and start all over again. Getting so secure in your pattern of life that you "don't have time" for anything new can be a symptom of apprehension. If you try something, you may like it, or if you don't succeed at it, you will feel like a failure. Have you ever thought of what you mean when you say you "don't have time" for something? It often means either that you *don't want* to do it or that you really are *afraid* to do it. Have confidence! In order to be successful, you should meet with success approximately eighty percent of the time. How can you have this success unless you try? Success does take creativity, you know: creativity with yourself and your personal resources.

Another important trait is tenacity. Put effort into what you think and do. Stick with it. Force yourself to work at your ideas. Have goals and work toward them with conviction. Take them seriously, but don't take yourself too seriously. You can always do better than you have done in the past, but work on yourself in the present. If you are tenacious about doing something, you will probably allow yourself the opportunity for creativity. This may sound strange, but creativity takes effort and discipline. It's not like gravy: it doesn't just "come." Keep at it!

Once in a while, even the best of us gets nailed on an idea we thought was terrific. Don't worry about it: your energy can be channeled in more positive directions. Keep your pride under control. What you can do at such times is to practice some self-preservation. In your own mind, play down your mistakes. Don't dismiss them, and don't deny them; just play down their significance if the situation appears to be wearing down your confidence. After all, nobody likes to be associated with a loser. So spend your time evaluating the situation: what you did right, what you did wrong, and what can be done to improve things. Don't second-guess! Accept what you have done, what has happened, and make the best of the situation.

Recognize the value of criticism, and when you give it, be sure it is constructive. Constructive criticism tends to be positive and usually elicits a better human response from the person who is on the receiving end of it. For example, suppose you have an idea that you think is great, and you tell someone about it who immediately says that it isn't good at all! What will you do? Of course, a defense of your thought is expected, especially if you had any hopeful thoughts about it. But will you try to find out why the other person doesn't like it and try to incorporate his or her ideas to improve your idea, or will you reject any constructive attempts to change because you believe that only *your* idea can be right in that situation? If you could lose some of your self-righteousness, you would see the good in constructive criticism. That is not to say that compromise is always desirable. If an idea is truly great, no compromise should occur. Fight it out! Try to, anyway.

PERCEPTUAL BLOCKS

Keeping an open mind sounds easy, but it often is not. No matter how hard you try, problems clutter your path. As mentioned before, tenacity and confidence will help you many times, but it always pays to recognize just what the pitfall is that seems to be blocking your way.

In the most obvious sense, perceptual blocks refer to a biological malfunction involving one or more of the senses that prevents an individual from using that sense. The person may be blind, deaf, or unable to taste, touch with feeling, or smell. It is necessary to live with, adjust to, and compensate for perceptual handicaps by means of increased sensitivity of the other senses. So blind people usually have more sensitive hearing than their sighted counterparts. In a way, they "see" with their ears and sense of touch. In the same way, how often have you "heard" with your eyes through lip reading?

If you are afflicted by one of the perceptual blocks just described, you and the environment can't communicate normally. Unless you make an effort to combat the differentiation, you may hinder your own progress. In this case, the "social" environment refers to the attitudes people have; the "physical" refers to objects and architectural features in the space.

PSYCHOLOGICAL BLOCKS

What about a more subtle but more dangerous problem than perceptual blocks? What about "psychological blocks"? Psychological blocks are ideas that society has ingrained in us, consciously or unconsciously. Values imposed upon you can influence your thinking, your hopes, wants, needs, and eventually, your own values. They can prohibit you from being free in your thought, not to mention your actions. Let's concern ourselves with thinking.

All design involves thought; therefore you have to be able to think. That sounds logical, doesn't it? It really is not all that easy, though. In order to design objectively, you have to be able to think freely, uninhibited by your deep, dark past. Don't let people tell you that something can't be done or that you can't do something. Just think of all the wonderful sides of life that we wouldn't know about if everyone had accepted these lines of reasoning: "If man were supposed to fly, he would have wings" and "If children were supposed to grow like weeds, they would look like them."

The key to coming up with creative, innovative ideas is to think without being inhibited. Think unconventionally! Just because an idea seems strange or weird or just different, don't throw it out. With a little help and confidence, it could turn out to be your best idea of the day!

You must also use ingenuity to detect what the real problem is. Otherwise, you are finished before you have begun. You might as well forget the whole deal. Consider the following problem:

> You are up in the wild, wild Yukon, and the place is infested with nasty marauding bands of brown bears, all ready to attack whomever is around. After hiding out all day in the tallest, thinnest tree you could find, you decide to do something drastic. You wait until all the bears are asleep, and then build a series of bear traps. Then, you go back up to your treetop hideaway and wait. When the sun starts to rise, you awaken, and wait until 8:15, when all the local bears are on their way to work. You count: five, ten, fifteen, two hundred, four thousand, eight million, . . . bears just coming out of the trees, skies, seemingly from everywhere! Suddenly, you begin to hear . . . shoop . . . shoop . . . shoop . . . shoop . . . shoop . . . shoop . . . shoop . . . shoop . . . shoop . . . shoopshoopshoopshoopshoopshoop . . . and then you notice that all the bears have disappeared! You have caught them all! You are a genius! You have caught eight million brown bears! Eight million *live, nasty* bears!

Now think about it.

Thought enough? Turn to Worksheet 3 and write your answers to the following questions:

1. Have you solved the problem?
2. Taking a hint from the reading, what was the real problem?
   a. You are a professional bear catcher who was behind in your quota of bears, and you had to catch up fast.
   b. You had to catch as many bears as possible.
   c. You had to get rid of the bears.

Let's analyze what happened. Actually, the immediate problem was solved because capturing the bears made the area safe. But you created another problem: what will you do with all the bears that you caught? The flaw in this solution to the problem is the conventionality of thought that precluded looking at the case holistically. The investigation considered only one aspect of the problem: how to make the area safe. What about "tomorrow"? No thought was given to what to do with the bears later, what would happen to the environment without the bears, and other similar questions.

The holistic approach to a problem, commonly known as a *systems approach*, allows us to look at problems from many different angles and disciplines. In the field of housing and interior design particularly, influences from art, technology, psychology, sociology, medicine, and physical education—to name a few subjects—are strongly influential and we must include them in the study. The *ecological approach*, which is also descriptive of the previous story, is the subject of the final chapter of this book. The following section gives a sneak preview of it.

SELF-SATISFACTION AND CREATIVITY: ANY CONNECTION?

Do you think that people become happier when they discover and learn new things? How does the feeling of accomplishment affect you? When you complete something that you doubted you could do, doesn't your "self-satisfaction" level rise, just a little?

Accomplishments are not to be taken lightly. Everyone needs confidence, and becoming proficient at something is a terrific way to attain that self-confidence. For now, though, let's talk about inquisitiveness.

Have you ever watched children investigate things with seemingly insatiable curiosity or listened as they countered each of your answers to the wonders of the world with a "why"? Children are naturally inquisitive, at least until society, first in the form of adults, tells them that they should be more accepting and tolerant and not question everything. The purpose of this section is to create within you a resurgence of this exploratory nature. In order to be a creative person, you have to question, investigate, and experiment before you can either conceive or propose a new alternative or accept the existing situation. These actions all require taking yourself less seriously than usual so that you don't feel like a fool when you do something that might be considered unconventional by others. After all, at one time or another people laughed at Henry Ford, the Wright brothers, and even Sigfried Mishbaum, and look at how all of them have turned into household words now.

You are not encouraged to revert to "kid-dom" just to regain some of your kid-like qualities. Abraham Maslow identified a number of basic human needs, ranging from the physiological needs of food, liquid, shelter and sleep to the growth needs, which include beauty, meaningfulness, order, justice, truth, and goodness, among others. Sandwiched in between these extremes is the desire to know and understand—in essence, curiosity.

Curiosity is a recognized behavior of all animals, children, and psychologically mature adults. All are intrigued by the mysterious: the experience of pursuing one's own curiosity leads to self-satisfaction and happiness. Repressing an inquisitive nature can produce boredom, disinterest in life, depression, and low self-images in previously healthy adults. These outputs can become extremely serious and also self-destructive if not remedied.

Especially desirable in the necessarily creative field of design (in engineering, industrial design, and environmental design, as well as aesthetic design) is curiosity, but its fulfillment is also a requirement of an emotionally mature person.

Some people are not afraid to express their ideas. In 1975, the *New York Times Magazine* ran an article on what "government would be promoting right now if it seriously believed in the energy crisis." Some of the suggestions follow:

Bedtime saving time. Does anybody really know why we switched to daylight saving time? It transferred an hour of winter darkness from pleasant evening to dreary morning. We light the candle just as long, but now we curse the darkness, too. This change makes sense only if the Government makes everybody stay in bed an hour longer.

Instead of eight hours of sleep, we would have to get nine, which is not a bad idea if you belong to the school that believes the country would be better off if everybody relaxed more. The school that believes all the terrifying medical views in the daily papers might argue that the country would be worse off, in view of a recent news story that people who sleep more than eight hours a night are prone to suffer strokes.

The government has to be heartless about this kind of problem, however. Moreover, it can always produce a statistician willing to prove the high stroke rate caused by the nine-hour night will be easily offset by the decline in the highway accident rate caused by lowering speed limits to 55 miles an hour. The Carter Government has just such a statistician at hand. He is the man who gets up the monthly forecasts that stability is just around the corner. . . .

Gas-pump tax audit: The Government's 10-gallon-a-week limit should be abandoned. It creates panic psychology which compels drivers to waste gasoline driving around in search of pumps to replace the gasoline they will have to waste tomorrow driving around in search of pumps to replace . . .

A sense of normality must be restored at the filling station. The present system converts the gas tank of the American family car into a hoarding place for vast gasoline surpluses.

This will be easily stopped if Internal Revenue assigns every filling station, say, a hundred daily notices to be issued to gasoline buyers in accord with a computerized random-distribution system. These notices would say: "Congratulations! A computerized random-distribution process has selected you for special tax audit by the Internal Revenue Service. You will appear at the examination room at dawn tomorrow with enough clothes for a three-day stay. Next-of-kin must not be notified of your whereabouts."

Very soon, people without real need for gasoline will stop driving into every gasoline line in town, and the lines will vanish, and filling stations will go back to keeping decent hours.[1]

[1] © 1975 by The New York Times Company. Reprinted by permission.

Similarly, *Time* in 1975 reported on an Arco advertising campaign that asked for solutions to the mass transportation problem. Some of the responses follow:

[A man] suggested that ardent energy savers be allowed to ride "Bumper-Snatchers"— lightweight pedicabs that could be hooked onto the bumpers of gas-guzzling regular cars at stop lights or highway ramps for a free ride. Another Californian, Mick McMick, urged that Los Angeles be put on a "revolving lazy Susan" for easy access all around. John Cody of Lynnfield, Mass., proposed a suction-tube system to "zip" commuters from suburbia to their city offices. Ed Hunter of Dayton, Ohio, felt that giant sling-shots in the suburbs could catapult commuters into outsized baseball catcher's mitts downtown: "Use baby oil to keep the mitt soft," he advised.

A good many proposals, on the other hand, were serious and promising—or at least provocative. A sampling:

Jitney Revival. Some contributers voted for jitneys, cheap, taxi-line buses that pick up passengers at designated points and deliver them to their doors in the most convenient order. Once common, they were banned in most U.S. cities in the 1920's after intensive lobbying by the trolley industry.

"Fly Me" Buses. People would use buses more, suggested Mrs. Carmen Dinicola of Alexandria, Va., if they had FM radio channels and served coffee and food—"like the airlines."

Canal Commute. The open aqueducts and flood-control canals that snake to and through many cities might be used for commuter boats. Said LeRoy Louchart of Fair Oaks, Calif.: "I know I for one would enjoy a cruise to the office in the morning. . . ."

Numbers Racket. To encourage greater use of mass transit, several writers proposed a rolling numbers game every time they take the bus or subway, riders would be given a lottery ticket that would make them eligible to win cash prizes in weekly drawings.[2]

What do you think of these suggestions? Outlandish? Practical? It really doesn't matter. The important thing is that people used their imaginations and were not afraid to say what they thought. At least a few of the ideas seem feasible. Some may appear to be premature, but remember the stories of the Wright brothers and Sigfried Mishbaum.[3] Anything is possible! Imagine what the reaction was two hundred years ago when someone jokingly said that people could *fly* coast to coast. If someone did say that, he or she probably was confined to a padded cell in some obscure place, never to be heard from again!

CREATIVE PROBLEM-SOLVING TECHNIQUES

How did the people mentioned above come up with their ideas? You would have to ask them. One thing to remember is this: on the surface, they probably look like any average guy on the street. Creativity inhabits those in whom you least expect to find it—even yourself!

In this section we are going to investigate several creative problem-solving techniques. Each one is simple and guides you through its path completely. These are all *design tools*

---

[2] Reprinted by permission from *Time*, The Weekly News magazine; Copyright Time Inc. 1975.
[3] Sigfried Mishbaum is a fictitious character.

that will assist you in eliciting information that you can use to solve particular problems. As you will see in Chapter 5, these creative design tools are an essential part of your design arsenal.

There are hundreds of design tools. A few of the more productive ones in the design sense are detailed here. For each, read through the description, then finish the problem as it has been presented.

Alphabetical Listing

This is a very direct way of suddenly having twenty-six or more ideas—some novel, some mundane—that pertain to your subject. Start by listing all the letters of the alphabet. Then, for each letter, list a word or phrase that begins with that letter and somehow seems to pertain to the problem you are attempting to solve. For example, consider this problem: "designing an elementary school classroom." The key word is "classroom," so you would write that at the top of the page. Below it you would write the alphabet. Leave space beside each letter to write a word or short phrase.

CLASSROOM

A—alternative	J—jump	S—supportive
B—beautiful	K—kindergarten	T—television
C—comfortable	L—library	U—unique
D—diverse	M—motivating	V—ventilation
E—efficient	N—neutral	W—windows
F—flexible	O—outside	X—xylophone
G—green	P—privacy	Y—yellow
H—hungry	Q—quiet	Z—ZZZZZZ (sleep)
I—individualized	R—rug	

After you finished your list, you would select several or all of the words or phrases and combine them into a total description; for example, "A supportive environment for kindergarteners would be diverse. It should be a space that motivates but allows for privacy, quiet individualized learning, and sleep, along with group activities. Design features are an integral component: yellow and greens can be either stimulating or restful, a rug may be good for controlling noise in areas where floor play is taking place." Some of it may sound crazy, but that doesn't matter. Now try it yourself. Using the preceding list, concoct your own design statement: _____

_____

_____

_____

_____

Functional Visualization

Instead of thinking about what an object will look like, think about what function it will perform. Think about function in the most elementary sense:

> can opener—removing the contents from a can
> lawn mower—method of shortening grass
> newspaper—method of transmitting information
> automobile—_____
> _____—_____

Functional visualization is especially helpful in the design of new solutions to old problems, which is a big part of design. Thinking of "removing the contents from a can" instead of designing a new can opener allows you to be less inhibited in your imagination. To begin with, you can ignore the traditional can opener and the traditional can. Perhaps a solution would be a self-opening can, which would eliminate the can opener as such. Most of design, remember, involves re-solving traditional problems in better ways. Functional visualization gives you many new ways to look at old problems.

Morphological Synthesis

Don't be scared by the name! This may well be the simplest technique mentioned here. Let's say we are seeking alternatives to the conventional chair. Like alphabetical listing, morphological synthesis involves making a list but in a more directed manner. First, you would write the word "seat" or "chair" at the top of a sheet of paper. Then you would think of several characteristics that describe the seat, such as: *materials*, of which seats are made; *shape*, which seats have; and *features*, which distinguish one seat from another. You would make three lists with one of these words heading each. Forgetting the word "seat" entirely, you would just list materials, shapes, and characteristics randomly as you could think of them:

SEAT

Materials	*Shape*	*Characteristics*
wood	round	folding
canvas	square	stacking
aluminum	angular	_____
rubber	_____	_____
_____	_____	_____
_____	_____	_____
_____	_____	_____

Then, you would choose one entry from each list and connect them. This would represent one solution. See how many others you can think of after filling in each of the columns with alternative words.

Example: an angular wood chair that folds

Your solution: _____

Inversion

Instead of thinking about how you can improve a situation, think about how you could make the situation worse! Or think about how to reverse it. Sometimes this process will increase your awareness enough to give yourself some fresh perspectives on the problem. For example, think of a traditional zoo where the animals are caged and people roam freely to see them. A more interesting solution is to "cage" the people in their cars and let the animals roam free. This idea creates a more natural setting for animals to live in, as well as for humans to observe. Can you think of another example? Write one here: _____

_____

_____

_____

_____

Bionics

The last technique to be discussed here deals with the question, "How did nature solve the problem?" Relatively recently, it has been discovered that the honeycomb, which is in the shape of a series of hexagons, is a very compactable shape, and it has been used as a housing form for people. The hexagon is quite a pleasing space, also, because it gives the appearance of spaciousness.

Can you think of an idea along these "bionic" lines? Write your idea here. _____

_____

_____

_____

_____

Description by Association

Instead of offering a description of something by recording what you read in a dictionary, associate it with something else, preferably something familiar. This is really not a design tool as such, but rather is a way of opening up your eyes to objects around you. In your role as a designer, it will usually be advantageous to you to be able to describe something with reference to another object that is similar to the one in question. This practice will simplify the task of your clients. They will not have to imagine to a very great extent what you are talking about. Basically, what you are doing is making the unfamiliar familiar. You can describe something that your client may not be able to picture with something that he or she knows well.

When a client says, "Well, exactly what do you mean by that, Ralph?" you have to be able to call upon a bank of stored descriptions to explain your idea. Remember, when people are spending their money on something, they want to know what they are going to get for it. It really helps to have a convenient method to aid clients' imaginations!

Practice this skill by describing some objects with which you are familiar and associating them with something else. For instance, given the word "doll," don't say, "plastic, twelve inches long with hands and feet." Say something like "a miniature person." Right away your client will picture what you want him or her to see. (Turn to Worksheet 4.)

Remember, there are hundreds of design tools similar to those mentioned here. Whenever you have a problem to solve, you can use one or several of these tools to free the ideas you need. Design tools can contribute to your creativity.

The information you can produce with these techniques will be useful in your design method, which will be discussed later in this book. Just keep all of the techniques in mind when you reach that section.

BIBLIOGRAPHY

Arnheim, Rudolph. *Visual Thinking.* Berkeley, Calif.: University of California Press, 1972.

Goble, Frank G. *The Third Force: The Psychology of Abraham Maslow.* New York: Pocket Books, 1975.

Hardin, Garrett. *Stalking the Wild Taboo.* Los Altos, Calif.: William Kaufmann, 1973.

Osborn, Alex. *Applied Imagination.* New York: Charles Scribner's Sons, 1963.

Papanek, Victor. *Design for the Real World.* New York: Random House, Pantheon Books, 1971.

Sommer, Robert. *Design Awareness.* San Francisco: Rinehart Press, 1972.

Stone, Christopher D. *Should Trees Have Standing?* Los Altos, Calif.: William Kaufmann, 1974.

CHAPTER THREE

VALUES

OBJECTIVES

Upon completion of this chapter, you should be able to:

1. Define and provide examples of human values.
2. Define human needs: physical, psychological, and social.
3. Relate, through comparison, human values to human needs.
4. Tell how and why values influence design decisions.

At times, people act according to seemingly instinctive patterns: they do things intuitively for reasons that they cannot readily explain. Everyone has basic feelings, be they conscious or subconscious, that act as lifelong guiding forces. Often these forces, called *values*, keep you on a familiar course, which may be beneficial or detrimental, when you are involved in decision making. Values do change, particularly during different stages in the life cycle stages, and some of them will change completely. But, as you will see, this process doesn't occur often. Values are long-lasting, and they are a necessary psychological crutch for all living things. Values give us a framework within which we build our lives.

Decisions, decisions. How do you make decisions? When was the last time you flipped a coin? Sometime in the past few years, you decided that you would or would not go to college. What prompted this decision? Record what you can remember below.

_____

_____

_____

For the time being, let's hold these thoughts in abeyance and examine values and decision making with regard to the physical and social environment.

Basically, *values* are affective feelings that you, as an individual, have. Values can be uniquely yours or they can be feelings characteristic of the society to which you belong. They consist of attitudes that you have developed personally or inherited. Values are your own thoughts and responses. They don't have to be verbalized. You may not even know that you have them.

Values are subjective. Their reason for being may be totally absurd and may even be founded in superstition. Often, they are terribly illogical.

Values affect all of our decisions, including:

HOW WE THINK AND DON'T THINK
BELIEVE AND DON'T BELIEVE
DO AND DON'T DO
NEED, DON'T NEED
ACT, REACT

Values are enduring. They take time to develop and nurture, and like anything treated with TLC, they are not easily disposed of or changed. Usually, once you've developed, inherited, been handed a value on a silver platter, or had one smashed on top of your head, you are stuck with it. There is really not a whole lot you can do about it. Sure, you can become a societal dropout, the black sheep of the family. But when you are fifty and looking back at your past, it may not be something you especially want to remember. Besides, the odds are that your far-out life-style was only superficial. You probably retained your original values throughout that entire portion of your life when you questioned your life-style.

Wait! Before we go any further, recognize that values are not all that bad. Sometimes they can provide an easy way out of a sticky situation. Suppose everyone you knew started cheating on exams, but you did not because you knew that your conscience would kill you if you did. Your personal value of not cheating makes your explanation easier because all you have to say is, "It's a personal value of mine not to cheat." Chances are that you will not be questioned further—laughed at, perhaps, but not questioned with any amount of seriousness.

What makes values so persistent, anyway? Well, people psychologically need values as a basis for their actions. Think of a time when something great happened to you and remember the feelings you had. Was the first thought in your mind, "Boy, just wait 'til my subconscious hears about this"? Of course not! At least, let's hope not, for your sake. No, you probably said something like, "Hey, Ralph. Guess what happened to me today?"

People like to share things, and they like to have a frame of reference when they are making decisions. People need *things* and ideas to relate to. These "things" can be physical, as in the security of a living environment, or they can be psychological feelings. All of these considerations contribute to a happier, better-functioning human being. Let's just hope that as a potential designer and innovator you don't end up being too logical and normal. That could be your doom, since you will probably be hired to produce something "different."

INDIVIDUAL VALUES

Simply stated, "values are motivative factors in human behavior. They provide a basis for judgment, discrimination, and analysis, and it is these qualities that make intelligent choices possible between alternatives. Values grow out of human interests and desires. They are the products of the interaction between an individual and some object or situation in his environment."[1]

Why do you desire things? Is it because of your culture, your biological configuration, or just your own personality? Human needs, whether they be physical, psychological, or sociological in nature, play a part in the determination of values. In interior design and housing, the psychological and sociological needs are hardest to determine because they are so amorphous.

Why do some people demand to have a showplace for a home, while others are content with a home that reflects their own comfort? Some people love spending time indoors, but others couldn't live without easy access to the outside: why? People sometimes cannot answer these questions for themselves, and for you to do it will probably be more difficult. Physical needs are the easiest to meet. You know what you are doing, whether it is providing for sleep, eating, or another basic function. But other needs are tougher to handle. It is easy to see how they are overlooked in human spaces.

Values are what goals are made for. Imagine describing yourself in this manner: you desire your ultimate life-style to be relatively uncomplicated, but productive, active, and extremely interesting. You want a comfortable, small, easy-to-care-for house in a quiet section of town; vegetable and flower gardens near an S-shaped swimming pool; and a brilliant red Mercedes 450SL so that your driveway will not feel lonely. The reasons, respectively, are these: you enjoy a peaceful existence away from the community's complications and prefer to go somewhere for services rather than be right where they are all congregated; you like working in gardens and seeing worthwhile results from your individual effort; physical exercise is important to your health and enjoyment; and it's a nifty car!

How do you think the goals of the house, gardens, pool, and car came to be? Certainly not everyone has these desires. All people are individuals and *value* different objects in life. Something happens along the way to influence a person to value a certain idea. For example, the remembrance of having little money as a child can provoke thriftiness in adulthood. A person who never really had a room for himself or herself as a child may regard the bedroom as a waste of space and prefer using it as an office or workroom instead. The absence of childhood privacy, which seems to be a cultural need (a need provoked by the individual's culture), can have varying effects upon people. These individuals may become obsessed with privacy or may lack a deep sense of the privacy desires of others. What are your values? Turn to Worksheet 5 and find out.

HOW VALUES INFLUENCE THE ENVIRONMENT

The environment can have a profound effect upon a person, no matter what age. An extreme case that is similar to the child who lacks privacy would be an urban living environ-

---

[1] Paulena Nickell and Jean Muir Dorsey, *Management in Family Living* (New York: John Wiley and Sons, 1968), p. 39.

ment where such crowding exists that no family member could carry out normal bodily functions alone. A person living in such circumstances is bound to acquire some type of value from this experience. Too often, crime results, but feelings of orderliness and cleanliness can also occur later. You can never predict human behavior. You can never tell how an event will influence someone. Research may provide some consensus of choice, but an offhand guess on the designer's part will probably be wrong and, therefore, is ill-advised.

Just in case you are still not sure what values are, consider this: What do you want to happen to you when you die? Wouldn't it be convenient if we all just disappeared—no mess to clean up, no major expense, and how ecological! But, unfortunately, this is not the case. Indeed, the American way of handling the problem can become complicated. You all know what usually happens. Relatives buy the "best," which probably includes an expensive, well-made coffin lined with satin and color-coordinated, with a soft mattress for maximum comfort. You would be dressed in their favorite clothes, fixed to look healthy, and admired by all in your "going-out" party. Finally, you would be placed to rest forever by a babbling brook or, if less fortunate, by a freeway exit, depending upon how far the good intentions (money?) of the family extend. Do you want this kind of send-off? _____

Why do you feel this way? _____

_____

_____

Suppose the deceased in question were someone other than yourself? What would you do and why? _____

_____

_____

So values make you do what you do. Think of a value you hold very dear. What is it?

_____

Have you ever thought about why you have this particular feeling?

Go back to the first page of this section. As a future housing expert or interior designer, you will be dealing with people on a daily basis. It's sort of like being a doctor, except that you are supposed to cure illnesses of a different type. Your belief is that the physical environment, when developed properly according to the situation at hand, can enhance people's lives, fulfill them and make them happier and healthier. Most times you do not know what your client's (patient's) problem is, so you must deal with that person on an interpersonal plane; you have to find out what he or she is willing to do to improve the environmental situation. Probably foremost, you have to be able to communicate well enough to determine the real problem. In this sense, a physician has it easy. If you have a broken arm, the trouble can be pinpointed and corrected. The same goes for a dentist: you explain that you have a toothache and you just know the problem will be found and treated, right along with at least thirteen other cavities you didn't even know about.

Your job often isn't that easy. This does not mean that physicians and dentists have it easy. The examples cited above are obvious and relatively simple to diagnose and cure. However, when you try to improve a person's living or working environment, you are working with minds and values. You have to be able to find out what people think and what they feel. This task poses a special problem, because even those most knowledgeable in the field do not know definitely which is more influential: the environment as a determinant of human behavior or people as determinants of the environment. In other words, a change in the environment *might* change a person's attitude, but how do you know it will? You can never be sure. And remember, how and why people acquire values is still a mystery. If people are abstract about what they *feel* they want, your task of creating a physical space for them is complicated. How do you know what to do?

Let's hypothesize that you have been called in by a couple who would like to spruce up their house. They tell you that they would like a total change: furnishings, wall finishes, floor finishes, accessories, lighting—the works. What do you think? Easy job, right? They have even told you that you can do anything you like and it will be fine with them! Here's the catch: they will spend only $2500. What about their values? What would appear to be an overriding value of theirs? _____

What does this attitude tell you about them? _____

Will you take the job?_____ If so, will you set any special conditions?_____

In this profession, you are spending other people's money, and everyone gets very touchy about that. Wouldn't you? You've got to be careful. You've got to be sure of your client and the ultimate goal so that you will be able to follow the proper course of action. So, you see, human relationships are very important. If you can speak with people and make them feel at ease, they will trust you more, you will feel better, and the chances will be greater that the job you do will turn out well for all concerned. How often have you felt that you trust someone because of the way that person looks at or talks to you? Little things count, and often they become the *important* cues in human behavior.

The living environment is deeply affected by human values. Often, construction of a house is viewed as just that: its construction. Nuts, bolts, hammers, nails, two-by-fours, . . . But it is much, much more. The housing environment rises, at least in part, upon human feelings: values, if you will. Just because something has not changed for an extended period of time doesn't mean it is out-of-date. Some designs are, indeed, *vernacular*. This means that their seemingly primitive form is actually as highly evolved as the present people and environmental conditions permit and require. Vernacular living environments most often satisfy people quite comfortably and completely. Their materials are indigenous to the area, and the physical arrangement of the living spaces is uniquely and adequately planned for the life-style of the inhabitants. The residents usually are well adjusted and desire nothing different.

We get into trouble in more "advanced" societies, where the burden of building is placed upon developers of large tracts of land. *Individuals* with good intentions usually are excluded from this profession today because of the extraordinary expense. A developer often is a stranger to the area in which the construction is taking place. Because of this circumstance and the pressure placed upon the builder to produce

the quality of life in the architectural products of the Modern Period, which codified most of the utilitarian/biological standards during the last half century, has been *less than satisfactory*. Traditional social networks (although some argue that they are anachronistic) are not accommodated; *aggregations of dwellings rarely respond to life-styles and cultural values* and the solutions based on logistical packaging, construction determinism or sculptural urban compositions, as well as the crusade for salubriousness have only offered *emptiness, uniformity, boredom and misfit.*[2]

It takes sensitivity, along with knowledge, to realize what you can change and when. Recognizing the values of an institution as large as a country or as small as the family can help guide your selection of an appropriate design. Misinterpreting information can lead to disastrous effects, perhaps to the creation of a totally inappropriate environmental solution.

HOW THE ENVIRONMENT INFLUENCES VALUES

Values can influence people's own self-concept. In design, it is a readily accepted fact that people will generally take better care of a space and its contents if it contains some extra comforting additions that normally are absent. For example, carpeting in a residence hall or office might make the users feel that those providing for them cared more about creating a pleasant place for them to live and work than just building a basic shell for their use. When people feel some extra comfort has been provided, they usually respond positively. In this situation, the values of both groups, provider and user, are apparent.

Publicly financed nursing homes give us another example of an institution that disregards human values. People who must move into these homes usually may not bring their own furniture with them. To many older people, their furniture represents memories and a familiarity with the environment that they especially need. It represents home: a building, people, and memories that are no longer with the individual. In old age, people often call upon *objects* to replace treasured aspects of the past, and therefore their possessions are essential. Being refused the companionship of their belongings at this time can be very disruptive to older people because their values may have become so tied to their belongings that without them they may question their reasons for living. For people who cannot actively continue their hobbies or other past pursuits life often becomes a matter of just passing time. Familiarity usually comforts them.

University residence halls also can enhance or diminish self-image. Lately they have become more sensitive to human needs. They provide a "sense of place," an environment where students can feel at home and where they have a relationship to the space. They allow for individual creativity. Many schools allow students to paint their rooms and put objects on the walls. Such personal touches are of extreme importance. Imagine if you were put in a room where you could do nothing to make it "yours." You just had to live with concrete block walls painted "institutional" blue, large windows with obviously worn venetian blinds, and dark, marbleized vinyl flooring. All you could do was bring in your own bedspread and pillows. You could do nothing to the floor or walls, and it is too expensive a proposition to buy a window treatment for such a short period of time. How would you feel? Would you feel you belonged there? Would you spend much time there?

[2] Hanno Weber, "The Evolution of a Place to Dwell: Anatomy of a Residential Site and Dwelling Design as a Participatory Process and Product," in *Designing the Method*, ed. David K. Tester (Raleigh, N.C.: The Student Publication of the School of Design, 1968), p. 130. (Emphasis added.)

The sterile environment described above can be likened to a prison. Prison life is said to contribute to the individual's delinquency to a measurable extent. If a prison is stark and impersonal, why do you think the inhabitant might degenerate during incarceration? Values. Confined to an environment that they cannot influence (personalize) because of its "hard architecture," people can react in different ways: by avoiding the place, if possible, or, in extreme cases, by destroying the objects within it just to prove that they do have some sort of control over their lives. Remember, the values we are dealing with are combinations of psychological feelings and the physical environment. We cannot easily separate them.

Lately, offices have been receiving some attention, too. Remember how frightening it was (maybe still is?) to go into the sterile, white dental office? This is one sight that has been known to provoke hysterical behavior in adults. But what if the office resembled a home instead of a hospital? True, you can't do anything about the medicinal smell, but what about the floors, walls, and furnishings? Carpeting, because of its psychological and actual warmth, can create relaxed feelings among people, particularly if it is in a relatively cool or low-intensity color. Earth tones are also appropriate. Carpeting will absorb and help diffuse sound waves so that you won't hear the screams of terror that might actually be emanating from the work room. And how about the furnishings? Can you think of any place more suitable to *anthropometric design* (objects designed especially for people through the determination of the population's average measurements) than a dental chair? If there is anywhere on earth that you need comfort, it's the dentist's office. And how about music? Music should be loud enough for you to hear but not loud enough to distract the doctor. Wouldn't it be awful if he or she got carried away with it and drilled your tongue?

You must recognize the implication here that the human values are evident in the physical environment. As a future designer, you should discover what will please people enough to draw them to a particular place and what will make them stay there. In most cases, the success of the venture will not depend upon that environment, no matter how special it is. Think about a restaurant: it cannot survive on a lively, unique atmosphere unless the food is good. The point is, though, that the environment does have an effect upon people, and provided all things are equal, it can improve the visitation or business of the establishment.

Values are just one aspect of design, but they are an essential consideration. They must be taken into account in offices, restaurants, schools, and probably most important, homes. Chapter 5, which examines methodology, will give you a basic procedure to follow when you attempt to solve a problem. Step 3c involves personal observation of a situation so that you can gain personal insight into the intricacies of it. This step involves values, and it is the place in the design paradigm where you will most likely determine and record them.

Now that you know something about the relationship between values and environment, find out some more about your own values by completing Worksheets 6–9.

BIBLIOGRAPHY

Barkley, J. David. "Room Space and Its Relationship to Mental Health: Some Observations of a Relocation Officer." In *Housing Perspectives: Individuals and Families*, edited by Carol Wedin and L. Gertrude Nygren, pp. 173-77. Minneapolis, Minn.: Burgess Publishing Co., 1976.

Deacon, Ruth E., and Firebaugh, Francille M. *Home Management Context and Concepts.* Boston: Houghton Mifflin Co., 1975.

Hardin, Garrett. *Stalking the Wild Taboo.* Los Altos, Calif.: William Kaufmann, 1974.

Horwitz, James. "Would You Believe It, Dying Could Be More Fun!" *Cosmopolitan*, November 1976, p. 222.

Koberg, Don, and Bagnall, Jim. *The Universal Traveler.* Los Altos, Calif.: William Kaufmann, 1974.

Malino, Emily. *Super Living Rooms.* New York: Random House, 1976.

Metz, L. Daniel, and Klein, Richard E. *Man and the Technological Society.* Englewood Cliffs, N.J.: Prentice-Hall, 1973.

Michelson, William. *Man and His Urban Environment: A Sociological Approach.* Reading, Mass.: Addison-Wesley Publishing Co., 1970.

Newman, Dorothy K., and Day, Dawn. *The American Energy Consumer.* Cambridge, Mass.: Ballinger Publishing Co., 1975.

Nickell, Paulena, and Dorsey, Jean Muir. *Management in Family Living.* New York: John Wiley and Sons, 1968.

Rapoport, Amos. *House Form and Culture.* Englewood Cliffs, N.J.: Prentice-Hall, 1969.

Simon, Sidney B.; Howe, Leland W.; and Kirschenbaum, Howard. *Values Clarification.* New York: Hart Publishing Co., 1972.

Sommer, Robert. *Tight Spaces.* Englewood Cliffs, N.J.: Prentice-Hall, 1974.

Stone, Christopher D. *Should Trees Have Standing? Toward Legal Rights for Natural Objects.* Los Altos, Calif.: William Kaufmann, 1974.

Weber, Hanno. "The Evolution of a Place to Dwell: Anatomy of Residential Site and Dwelling Design as a Participatory Process and Product." In *Designing the Method*, edited by David K. Tester, pp. 128-68. Raleigh, N.C.: The Student Publication of the School of Design, 1974.

Your Housing Expresses Your Values, Circular #HE530. Lafayette, Ind.: Cooperative Extension Service, Purdue University.

CHAPTER FOUR

SPACE

OBJECTIVES

Upon completion of this chapter, you should be able to:

1. Determine your own immediate personal space bubble.
2. Define personal space, territoriality, personalization, and privacy in the design context.
3. Identify and apply the physical, psychological, and sociological applications of human utilizations of space.

Before you actually design a space for people to behave in, it makes a great deal of sense for you to be aware of how they behave to begin with, doesn't it? Knowing what activities, conditions, and people you are planning for, you should be able to use your time and effort constructively and in a worthwhile fashion. Space, in every sense of the word, is our concern here, and this subject may possibly be the most influential aspect of the "analysis" stage in design problem solving.

As you read this chapter, maybe you will become aware of reasons for some things you do but never knew why. Or you just might notice some things you never knew you did!

PHYSICAL SPACE

Allow 54 inches for people to pass each other comfortably in a hallway.

Typewriter shelves should be three and one-quarter inches below a normal desk top height.

A desk chair's seat should normally be 18 inches off the floor.

The directives listed above represent perhaps the most apparent form of space: physical space. The previous chapter on values said that it is difficult to provide for the social and psychological needs that people have but that designing for their physical needs is quite a bit easier. Why? Simply because physical characteristics are a measurable commodity. You can measure, for example, how high storage can be placed in a kitchen by finding out how high a person of average height can comfortably reach. You can measure the furnishings that are being put in a space, add in the area needed for easy human movement, and learn the appropriate size for that space. Everything is concrete: you don't have to analyze people's feelings about the proper kitchen counter top height, for example. Most of these standards for building are already determined for you.

Space is to design what a foundation is to a building. Without knowledge of human spatial needs, chances are you will design inadequately for people. And since the physical needs are the easiest to isolate, we will discuss them first.

To begin with, there is a word in the preceding paragraph that is inappropriate in that context. Try to guess what it is, and put your answer here: _____ .
At this point, if you don't want to guess, you can defer your decision until later.

Anthropometrics is a word with which you should be familiar. Consider this:

It's ninety degrees in the shade. You get home from work after a particularly exhausting day, and you immediately go to the refrigerator, open the door, and find yourself looking directly at some icy lemonade. You get out your favorite glass, the one with the special handle that fits your hand, and pour yourself a glassful. Then you go into the bedroom and put on your coolest, most comfortable summer clothes. Now you feel ready to relax, so you go back to the kitchen to get your lemonade, then go out to the balcony to flop down in your favorite chair, the one you always felt was made just for you since it fits you so perfectly. The ottoman is also just right, and you put your feet on it. At this moment, you feel totally relaxed, as though everything in the world were made just for you so that you would feel comfortable.

Think about it. How do you think objects are designed? What is the physical basis of design for people, the designer's reference point? Raccoons? Of course not. People are. Before making any object for people, we must take into consideration the manner in which that object will be used. Then we can obtain the appropriate *average* measurements for reference. Specific human measurements are important in the production of objects for them. As an example, consider a chair. What measurement do you think determines the height of the seat? _____

What about the backrest? _____

What about the width of the seat? _____
The basic answers for all of these questions involve measurements. But in design we talk about "anthropometrics":

an•thro•po•met•rics (an' thro po met' riks) *n*—the measurement of the size and proportions of the human body

Anthropometrics is a pure discipline. Measurements are objective and scientifically obtained. Applying these measurements to produce a desired effect we call *ergonomics*, or the measurements of man implemented to accommodate him to machines. Anthropometrics is the tangible basis for producing optimum man-machine relationships.

In the story you just read, everything that was comfortable was designed *ergonomically* by the use of anthropometrics. Clothing, furniture, accessories; all are designed specifically for people as the users.

The physical space needs of people are most critical in the drawing of floor plans. These needs are measurable, and so as you will see, floor plans show physical spatial relationships. (Turn to Worksheets 10 and 11 and test your understanding of anthropometrics.)

There are other forms of physical space, too. In addition to the need for a certain amount of area around each person, everyone requires visual space: a place to rest the eyes. People prefer to rest their eyes away from other people. Indeed, it is a form of obtaining privacy for which you do not need to be alone. Just as you would not want a stranger to stare at you, neither would you want to stare at him for any length of time. For both people, the feelings this activity can create may be undesirable, for reasons that we are not always aware. What does it mean and how do you feel when someone you know stares at you? Of course, it depends upon the circumstances, but you cannot always identify your thoughts.

Designers cannot ignore the importance of visual space to a person's acquired sense of privacy. Even if the amount of space allowed to an individual is physically inadequate, barriers that visually provide privacy will afford some personal compensation. People can look around without feeling that others can see their thoughts. Just think what you can tell about a person by looking into his eyes! And how often have you been found out?

We must consider another form of perceptual space here. Even if the space an individual has is physically large enough and visually accommodating, noise can disturb people and give them a feeling of inadequate space. Excessive noise is a common occurrence. It can cause extreme psychological illness, insomnia, ulcers, heart trouble, and sundry other disorders. In addition, it diminishes the auditory sense itself. At a less severe level, it can provoke anxiety and feelings of insecurity in people who are continually subjected to this uncontrollable aspect of the environment.

Certain types of noise are all right. People can habituate themselves to sounds that are regular and of low intensity. For example, the indistinguishable background noise, called "white sound," that we so often hear in stores and large gatherings of people, usually causes no problems and, in fact, is necessary. But exposure to intermittent, high-intensity sounds, such as police and ambulance sirens and screams, for a long period of time may cause either physical or psychological damage.

PSYCHOLOGICAL AND SOCIAL SPACE

The areas that you will be designing must accommodate more than *physical* objects and *physical* needs. You were asked earlier what word was inappropriate in the paragraph:

Space is to design what a foundation is to a building. Without knowledge of human spatial needs, chances are you will design inadequately for people. And since the physical needs are the easiest to isolate, we will discuss them first.

What is the poorly chosen word? *Isolate.* Why? *Because all aspects of space are interrelated and interdependent.*

Physical space, or the ultimate environment that we see and use, should be determined through an analysis of human behavior and what function the space is to support. Human behavior is highly psychological and sociological. You don't just hug someone; a psychological feeling provokes you to do it. Someone doesn't merely hit another person; usually a psychological feeling will be behind it.

"Personal space" is largely a psychological concept. People are often unaware of their need for space around them. Like money, you usually only notice the effects of not having any when you truly *do not* have any. This "space" can exist in several forms, particularly in the physical and visual senses.

Physically, all people need a certain amount of space surrounding them in order to feel secure. The amount and shape of this space varies depending upon the individual and the activity. For instance, a person engaged in conversation with a close friend may feel quite comfortable with eighteen inches of space separating them, but this distance would be intolerable in a formal business meeting of two corporate executives. The spatial distances that people select can also influence the mood of the activity. A doctor who sits behind an imposing desk in an equally imposing executive chair and speaks to you as you sit six feet away in a smaller, obviously inferior chair, will probably convey a formal feeling to you, and as a patient, you may not desire to be treated in such a distant manner. The information you are about to hear from the doctor may be unfamiliar and disturbing enough for you to want a more personal approach. On the other hand, a doctor who chooses to abandon the security of desk and chair and sit closer to you without the barrier of the desk between you will usually make you feel more at ease. You may feel that you are being treated more as an individual than just another heart, broken leg, or tooth in a file. The absence of the desk as barrier, therefore, indicates a psychological as well as a physical closeness; it probably makes the patient feel important to the physician, thereby possibly improving their communication and understanding. So you see, the proper, sensitive use of space can affect human behavior in a positive manner.

On the other hand, close contact with other people can have negative effects. Consider the following:

Right now, think of yourself being in an elevator at your favorite local department store. You are the only person in this elevator. Everything is fine; you leave the first floor on the way up to the eighth floor. You have enough room to stand comfortably, and you find that you do not touch anything else even when you move. You feel totally at ease, knowing that this small, vertically moving bit of space is your castle. Alone, at last! Safe! But then disaster strikes! As you ascend, you find the elevator stopping, and to your utter dismay, what happens? Another person gets on the elevator at the third floor. What nerve! The audacity! This person just seems to have assumed that you either don't exist (after all, did he look at or speak to you?) or that you don't mind if your personal space rights are violated. You tell yourself to calm down since this really isn't your castle, much less your own elevator and anyone can use the space inside it. Besides, this intruder appears harmless enough, and you decide that sharing the elevator won't be so bad. The elevator doors close, and you are once again on your way. Everything is fine—didn't the new guy just smile at you? I think so. Just before the two of you looked up above the doors to see what floor you were passing. Or were you looking up there to make sure the elevator didn't reach the fifth floor before the fourth floor? *Oh, no! It's happening again!* At the seventh floor, the elevator stops, and this time five people enter. What a hostile-looking bunch. You decide to take refuge in the corner of the elevator, only to take one step back and find that you are already in the corner! What will you do? Looking around frantically, you decide to again look up above the door, an activity that seems to be very popular at the time. (How many others in the elevator do you find doing the same thing?) The door closes, and suddenly you realize that your time has almost come: the eighth floor is next. You have to get out, but how? All these *strangers* are in front of you, and they are all hostile, at that. The door is opening . . . now it's totally open. There you stand. You have to make your move. No one else is getting off! They're just standing in front of you! Don't they realize that this was *your* elevator before it was *theirs*, and therefore you have more rights than they do? What's wrong with them, anyway? Fortunately, the elevator remembered your desire to stop at the eighth floor, and now it's all up to you. So why are you frozen in the corner? Don't let all these people intimidate you. One good *push* would do it. Ready? You rear back, take a step forward, look menacingly at the head of hair in front of you, and as threateningly as possible, you say a very discrete "excuse me, please." The hair turns around, recognizes you as another member of the human race, and, after scrutinizing you, moves aside. You are lucky this time in that, as hostile as this group seems to be, it also moves aside for you, and you leave the elevator unharmed.

Has this ever happened to you? Although this case perhaps is a little dramatized, have your own experiences made you have feelings similar to those described above? The next time you find yourself in such a situation, keep track of what happens and make mental notes of how you act. Maybe your actions will be the same.

At times, other people just seem to get too close to you and you begin to feel uncomfortable, although you may not always know precisely why. The concept of personal space is, indeed, a personal one. Everyone demands a certain amount of space around them. Formality and informality imply different distances, for example. We can emphasize or imply formality by increasing the space separating the people conversing. Less space tends to convey informality. Intimacy shrinks the distance between people to inches. Each situation at the proper time allows people to feel very much at ease.

Inadequate personal space creates a sense of displacement and can be psychologically devastating to a person. Any animal, including man, must have some place or thing to call its own, no matter how large or small. One of the "human needs in housing" is a need for a sense of place, or *rootedness*. This primarily involves the person's emotional need to belong somewhere and to have come from somewhere. People require emotional attachments to physical objects and places if their future development is to be positive and progressive.

On a small scale, personal space involves the immediate area surrounding a person. Everyone has a *personal space bubble*, which we can define as the area around a person into which others are unwelcome unless invited. The size of this area varies, depending upon the individual and the culture. Certain cultures demand a large amount of space around their individuals, while others feel perfectly comfortable with comparatively little space there.

To picture this idea a little better, think back to a time when you were crammed in with a lot of other people, maybe on a bus or in a theater lobby waiting to see a movie. How close could another person come to you without your feeling uncomfortable? Did it matter whether that person was in front of you, in back of you, or to your side? If you can't remember, try this now. Find someone who will approach you from all of these

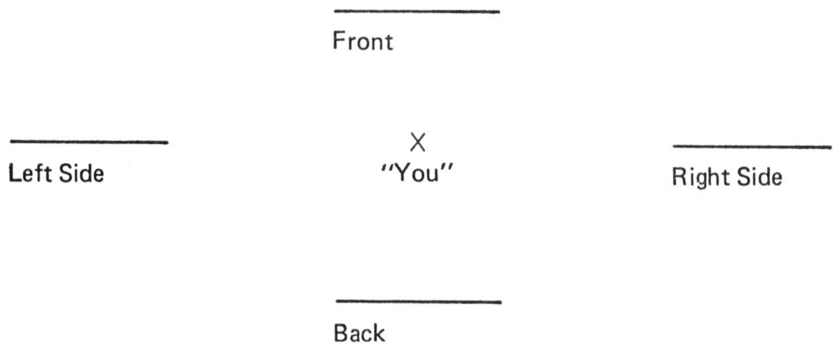

```
                        _____
                            Front


  _____               X              _____
    Left Side                "You"              Right Side



                        _____
                            Back
```

Figure 4–1.

directions while you stand still. Mark on the floor how close that person came to your sides and in front and in back of you before you felt threatened. Were the distances different? How? Use the spaces provided in Fig. 4–1 to record your findings. You are the "X" in the middle. Mark with a dot how close to you your friend was when you began to feel uncomfortable. Record the actual distances, measured from the middle of your foot to the middle of your friend's foot, on the appropriate lines. Then, draw a line connecting the four dots. What shape did you draw? _____

Which distance was the shortest? _____

Which distance was the longest? _____

What do you think this information indicates? _____

Most people can usually tolerate another person close to them so long as they are not face-to-face. Eye contact normally increases the comfortable distance, especially between strangers. How do you compare with the "normal"? (Before reading on, complete Worksheet 12.)

There are two other specifically designated forms of space that fall within the psycho-social framework. Both of them are related to personal space. *Territoriality* involves space that living beings declare their own. They indicate this ownership through their willingness to defend verbally or physically that which they feel is theirs.

Consider the case of the pet dog who, through barks, growls, and movements, admonishes strangers to keep a safe distance from *her* house and her people. The action of the dog is bound to say, "Don't come any closer; don't try it or I might bite you." The animal is bent on protecting her property and people.

The warning a suspected intruder gets may be more subtle. If you doubt the validity of a situation in which you find yourself, you may indicate an uneasiness to someone you perceive to be a threat by issuing a hostile look in that person's direction. Think about the universal situation where one person in a relationship becomes very jealous of the other whenever he or she pays attention to someone else. Behavior such as this can signify immaturity, insecurity, and a lack of self-confidence. Anyone who is sincere, mature, and secure in something will not behave in this manner. It is a passive attempt on one person's part to create a dominance over the partner, possibly by making the partner feel guilty about recognizing that others exist. The partner who falls for this ploy is being dominated through intimidation. (To be sure you understand the concept of territoriality, answer the questions on Worksheet 13.)

Another type of space is *defensible space*. This is an architectural interpretation of territoriality and personal space. People identify to others what they perceive to be their own through the creation of a physical barrier. Physical barriers can take many forms, but one we are used to seeing is a fence that surrounds someone's yard. Often this barrier means that intruders are unwelcome. If someone trespasses, the owner will feel obliged to defend the property in some way, like the nasty lady next door who screams at everyone who even looks like they are going to step on her lawn. Defensible space is a good example of how human behavior shapes the environment. (Now perform your own analysis of human behavior. Turn to Worksheet 14.)

HUMAN NEEDS

We have made several attempts to identify human needs. The chapter on values described the physical needs of sleeping and eating and also the psychological needs of privacy, security, and belonging. These needs affect spatial arrangements from the values standpoint and at least as much so from the space standpoint. Some of the most important human needs that affect interior design and housing will be discussed now. They are: belonging, knowing that you call a place yours and no one else's; personalization, being able to demonstrate your creativity in identifying some place as yours; privacy, having a place to go to or a method by which you can obtain time to yourself; and control, or a mastery over your life and environment. There are others, but this chapter will confine itself to these.

Belonging

Have you ever mapped out a place for yourself? In other words, have you ever felt that a particular place or object was yours and nobody else's?

All living things have a need to feel that they belong, and the ways in which they satisfy this need are diverse. Think of the cat who adopts a favorite chair and thinks nothing of staring down anyone who has the nerve, not to mention the naiveté, to sit there. Or the spoiled dog, the one who has been treated as a child, who has countless toys in a toy box, a special dog food cabinet, personal bowls and eating place, several specific sleeping places, and a feeling of unlimited "visiting privileges" upon her owners. Remove something important to her from her environment and she will feel disoriented since she needs to know her belongings will be there when she needs them. Without them, she, like people, will not have the necessary items to insure this feeling of belonging.

Having possessions is an aspect of belonging. Having space for these objects is the other, integrally linked, aspect. You can have one without the other. Think of traveling with luggage, yet never having a place to keep it, or moving into an unfurnished apartment when you have no furniture of your own. Human satisfaction is usually not complete under these circumstances. You need possessions and a place to put them where you know they will be secure in order to feel secure yourself.

So imagine yourself and what you believe to be a very safe position. Perhaps think about your home, car, or favorite chair. Picture it suddenly unavailable, either because it has been destroyed or because another person took it from you. What is your reaction? How do you feel? Let's say that you always sit at a certain place at the dining table, but last night a visiting cousin, one you don't appreciate very much anyway, inadvertently sat there. What do you think you would have done? How would you have felt? Chances are your answers to "doing" and "feeling" will be quite different. You might not do anything except tolerate the situation, but you might feel disoriented, forgotten, and perhaps unimportant since you might think that no one really cared about your place at the table. Not all living beings would react this way, but it would not be uncommon.

How often do you move and constantly find yourself thinking to yourself or talking to others (or to yourself?) about the place where you just spent time? The places of previous human habitation have strong influences upon those individuals. The memories of these places tend to polarize. Recollections either become better or worse than the experiences actually were and thus intensify feelings and accentuate the mental importance people allocate to their space, particularly their residential space. Try to think of a time when you have been a victim of this syndrome.

Personalization

Personalization is another important aspect of space. Through it, a person can create an awareness among others that a certain area or object belongs to him, and therefore, it should be respected as such. The tampering with or destruction of the area or object will be met with hostility by the owner. Have you ever had this experience? Have you ever returned to your room or personal space and found it all changed from the way you kept it?

Personalization also means imprinting personal values upon something, thus making it a part of oneself. It allows the emergence of creative urges so often inhibited by society. People do not personalize everything, only those things that they feel are theirs. For example, young people living in a communal arrangement will not personalize the living area that is used commonly by all of the residents, but they will decorate their own spaces in a highly individualized manner, conspicuously placing objects that reveal who they are. From a look at such a room, a stranger could probably tell quite a bit about its owner's personality or at least what that person would like to have the world see. The *portrayal and presentation of self* are extraordinarily important aspects of personal expression.

Privacy

Everyone needs to spend time alone. The lack of this opportunity, as Chapter 3 indicated, can have disastrous psychological effects. Lack of it can contribute to delinquency, crime, and passivity.

The opportunity for privacy allows you to discover yourself. It gives you time to think for yourself and by yourself. Maybe it gives people a basis for being comfortable and satisfied with their lives. Usually, unless you are secure within yourself you will have difficulty being secure with other people or in outside situations. A basically secure, happy person has more to offer others and the world than one who needs assurance and depends upon someone else for happiness. Always taking and not being able to give much take their toll after a while. Basically, privacy allows people to find out about themselves, to develop, and to become individuals.

Control

Control over the environment is one aspect of survival that is absolutely necessary for a person's self-concept and maturation. If people feel they are losing or have lost control over their lives or environment, psychologically their ability to function every day can suffer. Irreparable harm may occur. Just having a space, a personal space that you can influence and call your own seems to be essential for human growth. How can people feel satisfied if nothing they do remains as they left it? People must be able to know they can influence (change, adorn, personalize) something or someplace so that they can have confidence in themselves. This is all part of developing a good self-image. Loss of control over what happens to and around you might cause you to slowly give up lifetime goals and ambitions for lack of the necessary confidence to function effectively.

All of the concepts mentioned here are integral, supportive aspects of human needs in the spatial sense. Of course, there are more alleys to investigate both from the direction of human needs in housing and from the behavioral basis for all design. The bibliography gives some references for further exploration in this area. Worksheet 15 will help you to relate the principles in this chapter to interior design.

BIBLIOGRAPHY

Barkley, J. David. "Room Space and Its Relationship to Mental Health: Some Observations of a Relocation Officer." In *Housing Perspectives: Individuals and Families*, edited by Carol Wedin and L. Gertrude Nygren, pp. 173-77. Minneapolis, Minn.: Burgess Publishing Co., 1976.

Calhoun, John B. "The Role of Space in Animal Sociology." In *Environmental Psychology, Man and His Physical Setting*, edited by Harold M. Proshansky, William H. Ittelson, and Leanne G. Rivlin. New York: Holt, Rinehart and Winston, 1970, pp. 195-201.

Cooper, Clare. "The House as Symbol." *Design and Environment*, vol. 3, no. 3 (Fall 1973).

D'Atri, David A. "Psychophysiological Responses to Crowding," *Environment and Behavior*. Beverly Hills, Calif.: Sage Publications, March 1976. Pp. 111-25.

Denton, Trevor. "A Matter of Self Presentation at Home." In *Human Needs in Housing: An Ecological Approach*, edited by Karen Nattrass and Bonnie Maas Morrison, pp. 176-79. Millburn, N.J.: R.F. Publishing, 1975.

"Dimensions of Experience." *Design Quarterly 96.*

Hall, Edward T. *The Hidden Dimension.* Garden City, N.Y.: Doubleday and Co., 1966.

————. "The Madding Crowd: Space and Its Organization as a Factor in Mental Health." *Landscape*, Autumn 1962.

Lindsay, Peter H., and Norman, Donald A. *Human Information Processing.* New York: Academic Press, 1973.

Montgomery, James E. "Impact of Housing Patterns on Marital Interaction." In *Human Needs in Housing: An Ecological Approach*, edited by Karen Nattrass and Bonnie Maas Morrison. Millburn, N.J.: R.F. Publishing, 1975.

Morgan, Clifford T.; Chapanis, Alphonse; Cook, Jesse S., III; and Lund, Max. *Human Engineering Guide to Equipment Design.* New York: McGraw-Hill Book Co., 1963.

Newman, Oscar. *Defensible Space.* New York: Collier Books (Macmillan Publishing Co.), 1973.

Panero, Julius. *Anatomy for Interior Designers*, 3rd ed. New York: Whitney Library of Design, 1973.

Proshansky, Harold M. "The Environmental Crisis in Human Dignity." *Journal of Social Issues*, vol. 29, no. 4 (1973).

Rapoport, Amos. "The Personal Element in Housing: An Argument for Open-ended Design." *RIBA Journal*, July, 1968.

Scheflen, Albert E. *Human Territories, How We Behave in Space-time.* Englewood Cliffs, N.J.: Prentice-Hall, 1976.

Shorr, Alvin L. "Housing and Its Effects." *Slums and Social Insecurity.* U.S. Department of Health, Education and Welfare, Division of Research and Statistics, Research Report No. 1. Washington, D.C.: U.S. Government Printing Office, 1966. Pp. 7-31.

Nygren, L. Gertrude. "Planning for Ourselves." In *Housing Perspectives: Individuals and Families*, edited by Carol Wedin and L. Gertrude Nygren, pp. 164-68. Minneapolis, Minn.: Burgess Publishing Co., 1976.

Sommer, Robert. *Personal Space.* Englewood Cliffs, N.J.: Prentice-Hall, 1969.

————. *Tight Spaces, Hard Architecture and How to Humanize It.* Englewood Cliffs, N.J.: Prentice-Hall, 1974.

Stokols, Daniel. "The Experience of Crowding in Primary and Secondary Environments." *Environment and Behavior.* Beverly Hills, Calif.: Sage Publications, March 1976. Pp. 49-86.

CHAPTER FIVE

METHODOLOGY

OBJECTIVES

Upon completion of this chapter, you should be able to:

1. Identify and execute the six basic steps in the design paradigm.
2. Organize a problem along a methodological sequence.
3. Solve a problem methodologically.

Organization—a valuable thing! It can help you save time, make better use of your time, know what you do with your time. . . . It can also tell you what you should be doing. How? Well, consider this: the purpose of this chapter is to help you first to identify a problem, next solve it through analysis, and then evaluate your solution. The key to this process is organization, and the design paradigm presented on these next few pages will guide you through the steps involved so that you will understand your problem, along with where you are and should be going during the solution stages. Not to be taken entirely separately from creativity, methodology builds upon that concept by helping to make the best use of the design tools you acquired in Chapter 2.

So, with the realization that a systematic method of problem solving will make your task easier, read and answer the following questions as truthfully as you can before reading the rest of the chapter. See if your responses tell you anything new about yourself.

1. How do you define "methodical"? _____

   _____

2. When you are confronted with a complex, many-faceted problem, do you attempt to solve it in pieces or as a whole? _____

3. Referring to question 2, why? _____

_____

4. Provide an example of yourself as a very methodical person and explain why you are using this example. _____

_____

_____

5. Provide an example of yourself as the antithesis of methodical: a very intuitive person. _____

_____

_____

6. Generally speaking, do you consider yourself to be basically methodical or intuitive? _____ Why? _____

_____

_____

7. Referring to question 6, are you happy with your methodical or intuitive ways? _____ Why or why not? _____

_____

_____

What do you think of yourself? If you were an employer, would you hire yourself to develop television advertisements or as an accountant? Some professions, naturally, require a personality that is highly directed toward creativity, someone who can produce idea after idea seemingly off the top of the head. On the other hand, there are occupations for which the highly organized, patterned individual is perfectly tailored. Then there are vocations that are best suited to an individual who is a fairly even combination of both intuition and methodology. Alas, the interior design and housing professions are in this category. You should be a jack-of-all-trades and master of all, too, as much as possible.

Interior design and housing has usually been associated with art, which is at the creative, or intuitive, end of the spectrum. And, to some degree, this category is appropriate. It is, to a high degree, a creative vocation. It has to be, as do any occupations that concern themselves with the improvement of life. How else do you do that if you don't develop new ideas? The question is this: once you have thought of a new idea, how do you go about developing it to its fullest, most complete extent?

We talked about creativity first in this book because it often is difficult for people to train themselves to think freely and unconventionally. When you can do that, then it is time to put some reins on the thought process so that you control and direct it. That is why methodology is a necessary subject to master within the theory of design.

No one can classify himself or herself as purely methodical or purely intuitive. To be totally one or the other would be quite difficult for anyone, and besides, your brain just doesn't work that way. Some people are *very* intuitive, while some are *very* methodical, but in each person you will find a little of the complementary trait. In the design professions, you must be a combination of the two.

As stated earlier, "methodology involves the systematic breakdown of a body of knowledge into its workable parts." With reference to questions 2 and 3, above, a methodical person, when faced with a complex, multifaceted problem, will solve that problem methodically, or in steps. He or she will dissect and attack the problem in a logical order. Imagine trying to eat an entire T-bone steak in one bite. Isn't it great that someone invented a way for us to cut it up so that we could eat it conveniently? You should do the same with a problem.

DESIGN METHODS AND DESIGN TOOLS

Any *design method* is composed of several *design tools*. It is important to understand that there are already thousands of design methods and more are being developed daily. (Whether you know it or not, you have followed or created a method at one time or another. Can you think of when and how?) It is the way you combine design tools that will provide you with an appropriate method to use in solving your problem.

The design fields thrive on problems. In fact, if there were no problems, we would need no designers, right? But then, this state of affairs would imply that there was nothing to improve, correct, or change, and we all know that this is not the case. Design takes many forms and pervades many professions, and it is from some of these professions, particularly science and engineering, that designers have adopted much of their systematic methodology. This brings us to the question you are probably wondering about: why use a method when solving a design problem, especially since people in design are supposed to be creative and unconfined in their thought?

Think back a minute to the elusive but oh-so-important concept of creativity. Remember the word "imagineering"? This word means that you let your imagination soar and then engineer it back to reality. In Chapter 2 you learned a bit about how to give free rein to your imagination, and now you are going to see how to engineer it back to reality. Again, you want to achieve a balance.

The organization of a problem from its discovery through its solution can spell the difference between success and failure. To brainstorm without recording your thoughts can be a waste of time. You may forget some valuable ideas. Challenges that you undertake are complex, no matter how simple they at first may appear to be. It is worthwhile to investigate all aspects of them so that you know their scope and your actual goals.

Problem solving can be a real chore for some people, possibly because they don't know how to do it. Anything new usually presents problems. At first glance, solving a problem methodically appears to be a tedious, complicated task, and it is. Success requires tenacity. But there are some hidden benefits to adopting a problem-solving method. Perhaps the most important benefit is that it forces you to identify the real problem. Next, it compels you to record your findings in an organized fashion so that you won't be tempted, literally, to jump to conclusions. Last, it provides an efficient mechanism for you to thoroughly think through your problem before you begin to produce a physical setting. In short, a design method is the vehicle you use to get a project from its beginning to its end destination.

A DESIGN PARADIGM

A design method can consist of any number or types of design tools. A design tool is any device through which you obtain, organize, or evaluate information. A series of different design tools produces a design method. Regardless of the specific design method you select, it generally includes the following steps:

1. Prestatement
2. Problem statement
3. Information
4. Analysis
5. Synthesis
6. Evaluation

The next few pages will take you through the complete process. Keep in mind that this is a written sequence, not one that is merely mental. It is much easier for you to write down your thoughts than to have to remember everything. The sample problems in the following sections will help you master each design step.

Prestatement

This is a statement of the problem that you, the designer, will have to resolve. It may take the form of your initial contact with the client, in which you learn what he or she thinks should be done. What you have to be careful about here is this: what the client perceives as being the problem, in fact, may not really *be* the problem. The input is valuable to you, but it is up to you, the designer, to assess the situation and determine the actual problem. Nevertheless a statement detailing what you have heard is a starting point. This statement could take the form of a quote from your source of information.

Example: Client says: "We don't have enough room for all of our good students, least of all these. We need to add to this building anyway. All we need from you is a regular room for the kids to learn in—thirty desks, chairs, and a chalkboard. Just tell us where to put this room, order the furniture for it, and we'll do it. Remember, too, that these kids are real *problems* for us."

An alternative to quoting the source would be to summarize what was said.

Problem Statement

Any good project solution will state exactly what the actual problem is, in no uncertain terms. But this step is not as simple as it sounds. True, this is the second item on the list of six steps in the basic design paradigm, and indeed it should be *recorded* there. However, you don't write the problem statement until *after* you have determined the problem. You must first proceed to step 3 and gather "information" and then you can state the true problem. If you try to write the problem without investigating all of the aspects listed in the "information" section, you probably will miss the crux of the problem.

Example: The school needs a space in which low-achieving students will feel motivated to learn and investigate. It should be away from unnecessary environmental distractions but near the other classrooms and students. The area should support a variety of classroom activities, including lectures, group discussions, and physical activity. Flexibility is highly desirable.

Information

This is the exhaustive stage at which you uncover all of the details that relate to your problem. This is the point at which you do the research: reading, observing, and scrutinizing. Some of these activities help to make research the most enjoyable stage, too. For instance, it is at this stage that you meet the people involved in the project, observe them, talk to them, and, sometimes, get to know them. It all takes time, but for part of that time you may be enjoying yourself so much that you won't want to go on to the next step in the design process! Record all of the information you will eventually use. Usually you can break down what you learn into three areas, as follows:

1. *Literature:* This category comprises a review of written material that pertains to previous problems similar, in full or in part, to yours. Record, document, and preserve all information that you discover, however minute, including written information provided by your client pertaining to the immediate situation, periodicals, pamphlets, books, and other literary sources. The simplest record is a list of singular facts that you have found. List *everything:* this list should be as complete as possible, even though the individual facts may number in the hundreds. Conscientious effort at this stage will make your work easier later, because all of the knowledge you use in your actual design solution will come from this list.
2. *Experienced persons:* Anyone you can contact, in written or verbal form, who can provide you with information helpful to your cause qualifies for this category. Simply add their names to the list already begun. Remember to write only single thoughts for each listed entry.
3. *Observation:* Your own personal observation of the present situation is essential in personalizing and validating your data. It provides you with intimate views of what your problem entails. No problem is exactly like any other one. Often you do not become aware of the individual, subtle differences in projects until you personally observe the situations. It is at that point that the personalities of individuals and corporations become evident and you find out how unique and interesting these people really can be!

Example: Randomly list the data that you have collected through the means mentioned above.

1. Good colors for concentration are pastel yellow, pink, green, and blue.
2. Small group discussions and lectures will occur in the space.
3. Outside distractions, such as noise, are undesirable.
4. Twenty-six students will be accommodated.
5. Carpeting will help cut down on noise.
6. Strong contrasts of colors will enliven the space.

7. Free space will add flexibility for furnishings and classroom activities.
8. The atmosphere must be conducive to learning.
9. The students are usually unmotivated toward learning.
10. Special teaching aids are necessary to attain student interest.

And so on, for as many bits of information as you find.

Analysis

Once you have completed your information search, you can begin to analyze your data. Strangely enough, the most beneficial first step here is to determine what the real problem is. A thorough investigation of the situation at hand will give you sufficient insight to ascertain the actual problem, as we discussed earlier.

Having written the problem statement, you can begin to sort through the data you have collected. Analysis of the problem involves deciding how you are going to attack it. Let's backtrack a minute, though.

So far, you have interviewed your client, ascertained the real problem, and collected all the data you can find relevant to it. Your job now is to manipulate those data into a solution. In this stage, you think through possible solutions. In a sense, this is a stage of trial and error, a step that gives you the opportunity to start and stop solving the problem over and over again. *Repeat: this is a think stage.* Do not conceptualize the total solution here. You should be thinking about the situation in parts (methodically), which you can later arrange into the order that you determine to be best.

At this point, please remind yourself that there are thousands of design methods. Let's say you are attempting to follow a particular method because you are familiar with it and it seems suitable to your problem. This course is perfectly all right. But if you should find yourself in the position where the design method does not appear to be as direct or convenient as you wish, do not hesitate to change it.

Getting back to the solution of the problem, remember to approach it in stages, a little at a time. Begin by looking back at the information you collected. Pull out several items that are related and form them into a group. This will become a "partial solution," which is actually the solution to one part of your problem. For example, suppose you have itemized all of your information; that is, each item pertains to a single aspect of your problem. What you should do now is to search for commonalities: find several items in the list that seem to be similar in some way. Then compose a unifying statement that incorporates these individual statements to form the partial solution. Continue this process until you feel you have formulated a solution for every aspect of your problem. Each partial solution statement may incorporate from two to five or so bits of information.

Next, look for commonalities among the partial solutions, compose more unifying statements, and call them "combined solutions." These will be quite a bit longer than the partial-solution statements. A combined solution will actually be a verbal description of the final decision you have made for a major aspect of that problem, if the problem entails more than one part. If it does not, then the combined solution will be the final project solution, but only *verbally*.

Example: Partial solutions
1. Carpeting should be placed where lectures occur so that the space will be quieter.

2. Strong color contrasts should be used where discussions will occur.
3. Audiovisual aids should be placed where the entire class can benefit from them.
4. Audiovisual aids that can be operated individually by each student should be provided.

Combined solution

1. Two classroom sections will be created: one for small group discussions will utilize contrasting color schemes; a lecture space will be painted a pastel color. For acoustical purposes, the entire space will be carpeted. Venetian blinds, allowing for light and visual control of the outside surroundings, will be installed at the windows. Audiovisual aids and other teaching aids will be available throughout the space for individual and group use.

You have read about, and presumably learned, how to think through a problem. The last step mentioned in the design paradigm, that of composing a combined solution from the information collected, allowed you to put together the design elements in finished verbal form. Here is a question for you: can you honestly say that you know what your own space will look like, based on what you have done so far? Do you know, in other words, what this proposed classroom will be like? Do you know everything about that space, including what functions will be performed where, with what, and how? If your answer is "no," you should feel *good*! You should not be able to do all of these things yet. You might be beginning to have an idea of your creation, but you should not know exactly how it will turn out.

Remember again what methodology is. Go back to the beginning of this section and copy the definition in this space: _____

_____

Now take a minute and think about this description. What does it mean? Of course, it refers to the dissection and solution of a problem in a step-by-step format that is designed to guide your project solution along sequentially. If you said that you already knew what your final space would look like, you are out of the sequence. You have jumped ahead. You are being *too* intuitive. Why? Because the complete analysis stage is intended to provide you with the opportunity to gradually formulate a finished verbal statement to serve as the basis for the ultimate construction of a solution. If you do not utilize this step-by-step procedure as it has been presented to you, or a method somewhat similar to it, you may miss some very important aspects of your project. Don't think that methodology makes mountains out of molehills: it helps you to thoroughly investigate your problem so that you have a better chance to create the proper environment.

Try your hand at analyzing another problem. Turn to Worksheet 16.

Synthesis

The next step in problem solving is the synthesis, the conceptualization of your project's solution in a graphic manner. Now you can make your visual materials and *show* what the final product will be. This may be the "fun" stage, the point at which you actually lay out spaces, select furnishings, finishing and construction materials, and so forth. Don't forget, though, that a lot of responsibility lies in this stage, and most of it is rooted in the analysis section of this design paradigm.

Remember this: even though using a design method may appear to be cumbersome, it really is something that makes problem solving and decision making easy for you. True, it takes time and discipline, but you will probably produce a better design if you methodically work through a problem. Intuition and creativity have their places in this framework. Do not forget them. Just use them wisely and to your best advantage—and *organize them*. Don't let your imagination block a design requirement. Here, again, artistic/scientific balance is necessary. This balance is something you will have to discover for yourself.

Example: All drawings, sketches, verbal descriptions, models, or other visuals that relate to the project belong here.

Evaluation

The evaluation of a project may take place at different times. You may do it *after* the project has been finished and has been in use for a while. By visiting the space then, you can very effectively judge your result and make whatever changes are necessary. This technique is a good one, because it allows you to change unsatisfactory aspects of the design. In most cases, at this stage there is no additional expense to the client. Here's the catch: there is an expense to you, so obviously, you had better not have a lot to change!

The alternative is to check your design *before* the actual construction of the project. This type of evaluation consists of a series of questions that you ask yourself, based on what you set out to accomplish. In each project, there are specific objectives that you must satisfy. Ask yourself questions based upon these objectives. Should you answer "no" to any of the questions, go back and see what you can do to change your answer to a "yes." All "yes" answers will more than likely mean that your solution will basically work. All design projects need to be changed at one time or another. You should aim to minimize the number of major changes that could occur due to oversight. You and your client both will be happier as a result. To evaluate a project before it is constructed, ask yourself questions similar *in style* to those listed in the following example. Each problem, remember, has its own personality, and your questions will change as the problem changes.

Example:

1. Does the space accommodate twenty-six students in both physically active and sedentary activities?
2. Is the space flexible?
3. Does the space contain a variety of teaching aids and areas?
4. Are outside distractions minimal?

SUMMARY

Solving a problem methodically will open your eyes to aspects of the project you may not have foreseen.

All of the topics mentioned in the first unit of this book belong in the design paradigm. They contribute primarily to data collection, to discovering as much information as possible.

Use any pertinent statement or finding as part of your solution. Methodology is an integral part of these topics because it organizes the information the other chapters have helped you to collect. Worksheets 17 and 18 should convince you of the importance of methodology—if you're still a nonbeliever.

BIBLIOGRAPHY

Davis, Robert H.; Alexander, Lawrence T.; and Yelon, Stephen L. *Learning System Design: An Approach to the Improvement of Instruction.* New York: McGraw-Hill Book Co., 1974.

Hill, Percy. *The Science of Engineering Design.* New York: Holt, Rinehart and Winston, 1970.

Jones, J. Christopher. *Design Methods: Seeds of Human Futures.* New York: Wiley-Interscience, 1970.

Mager, Robert F. *Preparing Instructional Objectives.* Belmont, Calif.: Fearon Publishers, 1962.

Metz, L. Daniel, and Klein, Richard E. *Man and the Technological Society.* Englewood Cliffs, N.J.: Prentice-Hall, 1973.

UNIT TWO

DESIGN
FUNDAMENTALS

OBJECTIVES

Upon completion of this unit, you should be able to:

1. Plan and graphically present a schematic drawing as a preliminary step in the physical-space-planning process.
2. Use an architect's scale, triangle, T square, and parallel bar in the preparation of drawings and lettering for projects.
3. Develop a style of lettering that you can execute well for use in the preparation of future projects.

A knowledge of human behavior and its effects upon the spatial layout of the environment and the effects of the environment upon human behavior are necessary prerequisites to the physical-space-planning step in design. An awareness of human behavior and its relationship to design prepares you to seriously plan spaces for human use.

The next step in the design process is to apply what you have learned about people and their behavior to the environment. Before beginning an actual drawing, though, there are a few preliminary steps to master. One of these, the schematic drawing, or bubble diagram, as it is sometimes called, allows the organization of the tasks in a space according to their relationship to each other. It shows approximately where different activities will occur in an area without giving a definite indication of the space's shape. The other two steps concern the visual presentation of the project itself. First, you need to master the basic drafting equipment. This proficiency is necessary so that drafting will be neat, accurate, and convenient to do. Using the architect's scale comes first, followed by the procedures for using the triangle, T square, and parallel bar. Lettering is the next skill to acquire. Mastering an attractive lettering style permits the communication of design ideas in an intriguing manner. It can add to the project's interest immeasurably.

After acquiring the skills necessary for these preliminary steps in the design process, you will be ready to start representing your ideas through actual architectural and pictorial drawings. These drawings are the subjects of Unit Three and represent the final step in the design methodology included in this book.

CHAPTER SIX

SCHEMATIC DRAWINGS

Having had some experiences with human behavior, you are ready to begin organizing the information you have gathered in the desired physical spaces. Remember, as explained in Chapter 5, you must explore a problem theoretically before conceptualizing it. So far, the basis of the interior design and housing subject area has been presented: the problem of deciphering what types of facilities and environments suit the situation at hand. Learning to find information to solve problems is an indispensable step in the designer's work as a problem solver.

A schematic drawing will help you to think. Just as methodology organizes random thought processes, a schematic drawing forces the designer to record information on paper so that it can be seen. Writing something down and looking at it always seems to make the true situation more realistic and easier to comprehend. You can imagine something, but actually looking at it often clarifies it.

To illustrate the place of a schematic diagram in the design paradigm (where it probably belongs to the analysis or synthesis stage, depending upon the specific interpretation of the design methodology used) imagine that a residence hall for university students is to be designed. You have come highly recommended for this job, by the way, because of your vast knowledge of what it takes to sustain yourself in strange places, having just recently been a student, too. At this point in your career, you are either a consulting housing expert who has studied the living environment needs of various groups of individuals or you are a member of an architectural or design firm that is part of a team working together on this project. *Think*, now. What will you do? Well, begin with the prestatement:

Q: What have you been told to do?
A: Design a residence hall for university students.

Then decipher the true problem statement:

Q: Is this just like any other residence hall?

A: No. No two situations are alike.

Q: What do I put down for the "problem statement," then?

A: You collect your information, then decide what the real problem is, remember? You come back to this stage after that.

(Oh, yes, now it's all coming back.)

So, let's go on to the information stage. For our purposes, imagine the activities a college room should support. Reading, writing, studying, sleeping, book storage, clothing storage, talking to friends, and watching TV are probably fairly standard "student needs." Just thinking about it, notice that some of these activities could take place in the same spot. But why imagine it? Why leave it to chance? Remember, a schematic drawing *clarifies* the thought process. So *write it all down and clarify* (or organize).

Begin by listing the activities:[1]

1. Reading
2. Writing
3. Studying
4. Sleeping
5. Book storage
6. Clothing storage
7. Talking to friends
8. Watching TV

Looking at these activities, begin to relate some to others. For instance, it may be that reading, writing, and studying have a relationship. Surely reading and book storage have some sort of commonality. Instead of just imagining, draw the relationships as you see them. Doing so will make the activities that are essential to each other and those that are independent become apparent. Draw lines linking related activities:

1. Reading
2. Writing
3. Studying
4. Sleeping
5. Book storage
6. Clothing storage
7. Talking to friends
8. Watching TV

What do we have here? Apparently there are two activities that seemingly have no relationship to any other. What are they?_____ and _____

[1] Take special note: *Activities*, not pieces of furniture, are the items of interest here. As outlined in Chapter 5, physical objects such as furniture and walls are placed in spaces only after the needs of the spaces have been thoroughly evaluated. In this chapter, activities are *still* the focus and not the drafting of a space in which these activities will take place. In the "idea representation" unit of this book, spatial limitations such as floors, walls, and furniture to the activities can be assigned. Only then, *not now!* For now, just think about it.

Talking to friends and watching TV, in this case, are related. In fact, it almost appears that two very distinct areas are going to result in this space. What are they?

Before exploring the answer to the last question, let's see what the schematic drawing will look like. At the beginning of the chapter, you read that a schematic diagram also may be called a "bubble diagram." Why? Because, in effect, the finished drawing looks like a lot of bubbles: you assign each activity to a bubble, which you draw around the activity. Figure 6-1 shows what the finished bubble diagram *could* look like. Just a bunch of clouds— or bubbles—right? Has this diagram occurred randomly, or is there a reason for the size and placement of each bubble? By now it should be clear that almost nothing occurs randomly.

Figure 6–1.

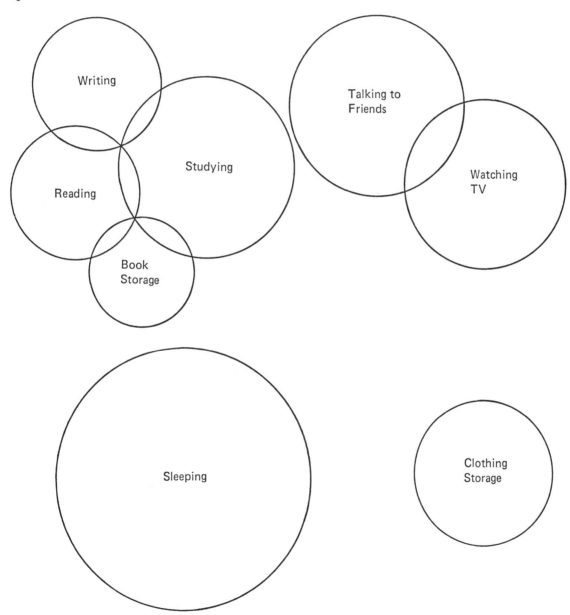

There most certainly is a method to all this madness. An activity that stands in a circle by itself does not have a strong relationship with another activity and it probably will have its own place in the designed space; no other activity will occur there. Two activities that overlap each other have a definite relationship and in all probability will share some of the space's facilities. "Talking to friends" and "watching TV" are examples. These two activities tend to be noisy and may occur in a distinct area. Writing, reading, studying, and book storage have relationships to each other, as indicated by their interlocking bubbles. They tend to be quiet and so apparently form the other distinct area in the space.

Schematic drawings show three things: the *relative* size, shape, and placement of activity spaces that the design must accommodate. The important word to remember here is "relative." The bubble diagram gives no idea, for example, of how many square feet

Figure 6–2.

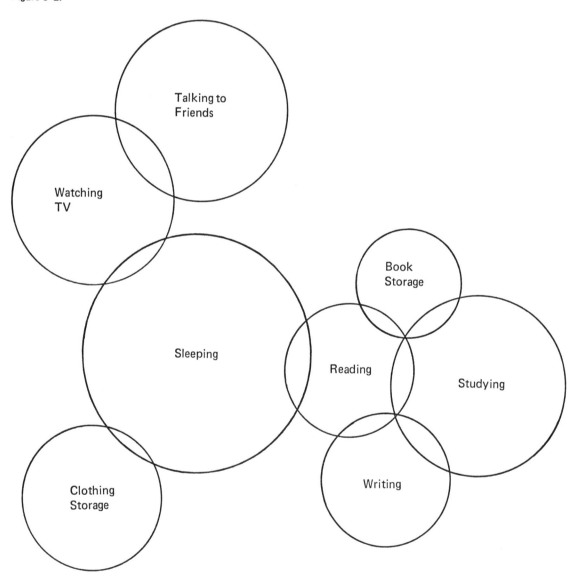

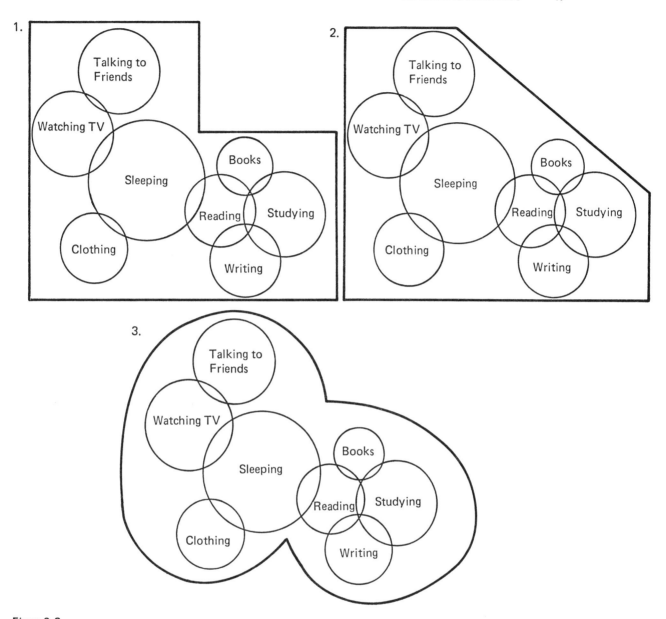

Figure 6-3.

to allot to the "talking-to-friends–watching-TV" area. Notice, though, that this space is larger, relatively speaking, than the "reading–book-storage–writing–studying" area since the bubbles representing these activities are, in total, larger than the other space. In a schematic drawing, *everything is relative.*

Looking at Figure 6-1, try to determine what other relationships it shows. Some are already distinct, but what about "reading" and "book storage": is there a direct relationship? How about between "writing" and "studying"? "Writing" and "book storage"?

You should realize that any number of schematic drawings can result from a list of activities like the one given in this chapter. A different interpretation could change the entire drawing around. For example, compare this set of relationships to the earlier list:

1. Reading
2. Writing
3. Studying
4. Sleeping
5. Book storage
6. Clothing storage
7. Talking to friends
8. Watching TV

In this case, the schematic drawing would possibly resemble Figure 6-2.

We can indicate the relative shape of the resultant space by drawing an outline around the bubble diagram. For instance, the schematic drawing in Figure 6-2 could take any of the shapes shown in Figure 6-3.

In addition to being a design aid for you, a schematic drawing can also be an attractive and informative addition to your final project presentation. All you have to do is be more careful with it, make it neater, use ink instead of pencil, maybe add color to it, and letter it attractively (Chapter 8 discusses lettering in detail). As part of a project presentation it will show the client how you determined the spaces in the design proposal. Any visual aid will help immensely in the explanation of the project.

Worksheets 19–22 at the back of the book will help you to implement the ideas from this chapter.

CHAPTER SEVEN

USING BASIC DRAFTING EQUIPMENT

Have you ever seen an architect's blueprint drawings? Did you ever wonder how they became so accurate, so perfect, so professional? Things like that usually do not happen by accident. No one yet known to civilization has been able to sit down and free-hand a great set of architectural drawings. It takes practice, patience, and technique.

This chapter will tell about some of the devices that will help with drafting. It will become apparent that there is an almost infinite number of gadgets that will aid in the production of design visuals. This is an introduction to these tools. The ones that are discussed here are the most indispensable pieces of drafting equipment.

THE ARCHITECT'S SCALE

The architect's scale is a tool of the design trade. A ruler of sorts, it simplifies the task of representing large, life-size spaces on pieces of paper that you can carry around conveniently.

An architect's scale has three primary surfaces. In all, twelve different "rulers" are on it. To begin with, look for the number "16" at the ends of the scale. This number identifies the familiar foot ruler. The remaining sides of the scale are probably a little foreign right now. Look for the number "1" at the ends of the scale. Find it? This scale is the "inch" scale; in other words, one inch on this scale represents one foot in reality. So if we wanted to represent eleven *feet* in real life in one-inch scale on a piece of paper, we would draw a line eleven *inches* long.

Look again at the inch scale. How does it work? Right next to the "1," you will see the first *true inch* marked off in tiny segments, perhaps as shown in Figure 7-1. What this is is simply a miniature foot ruler. On an inch scale each actual inch is divided into twelve parts, which represent the twelve inches in a foot. Remember, in this scale, the inch represents one foot.

Each segment represents one inch

Figure 7-1.

Now look one inch to the left or right of the first inch, depending upon where the "1" is. You will see the number "2," and one inch further will be the number "3." These stand for "feet." A line representing a distance of three feet, six inches, in one-inch scale is shown in Figure 7-2. See how it works? Start the line by drawing the inches first, followed by the feet. It may seem backwards, but it should prove to be easy.

Figure 7-2.

All of the scales work the same way. Look for the fraction "$\frac{3}{8}$" at the end of the scale. On this scale every three-eighths of an inch represents one foot in reality. Appropriately enough, this scale is the "three-eighths-inch scale." A three foot, six inch line in this scale would look like the one in Figure 7-3.

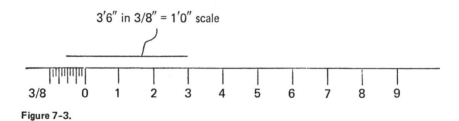

Figure 7-3.

It's really quite simple, and there is a wide choice of scales from which to choose. Look at the ends of the scale again. Each of the numbers that appears there represents a particular scale: 3, $1\frac{1}{2}$, 1, $\frac{1}{2}$, $\frac{1}{4}$, $\frac{3}{8}$, $\frac{3}{16}$, $\frac{3}{32}$, and so on. Which scale you select depends upon the size of the space you want to draw. Generally speaking, the larger the space, the smaller the scale. Scales represented by the larger numbers ($1\frac{1}{2}$, 1, $\frac{3}{4}$, and $\frac{1}{2}$) are large scales, while smaller numbers ($\frac{3}{8}$, $\frac{1}{4}$, $\frac{1}{8}$, $\frac{3}{16}$, and $\frac{3}{32}$) are small scales. Why? Think of it this way: eight feet drawn in inch scale would make a line *eight inches* long. But in one-eighth-inch scale, the line would be only *one inch* long. Try this on the architect's scale and then complete the exercises in Worksheet 23.

How does the size of the space to be drawn affect your choice of a scale? Well, a designer must shrink a large area much more to begin with than a small one so that the drawing will be easy to look at and handle. So, for a small single room the inch or half-inch scale would be an appropriate choice. If a large restaurant's dining room were the subject, the one-eighth-inch scale would be a more reasonable choice. It's all relative.

THE T SQUARE

The T square is an instrument that helps to draw straight, horizontal lines. It is called a "T square" because it is shaped like the letter "T." The part that forms the crossline is designed to fit over the edge of the drafting surface so that when you slide the T square up or down, the elongated plastic-edged arm will remain parallel to the top and bottom edges of the work surface. This property facilitates the drawing of lines that are horizontal, straight, and parallel to each other without excess measuring.

Developing an affection for the T square will not take very long. True, it may not look like something you would normally get excited over, but give it a chance! Right now, take out a piece of scrap paper, a pencil, and a ruler. Draw a two-inch square on the paper. Make sure that each side is two inches long, and also be sure that the resulting figure is a square and not a parallelogram. Oh, yes . . . *time yourself*. Finished? How long did it take? Write the time here: _____. Don't be discouraged, but whatever your time, it's *too long*! The T square will help you draw such figures better and faster. How? Read on.

First, tape your paper to the drafting surface. Place one piece of tape at each corner of the page. The tape will prevent the paper from slipping during the drawing process. Next, take the T square and place the plastic-edged arm horizontally on the work surface, slipping the crossbar off the right- or left-hand edge of the surface. Fit it tightly against the edge, as illustrated in Figure 7-4.

Figure 7–4.

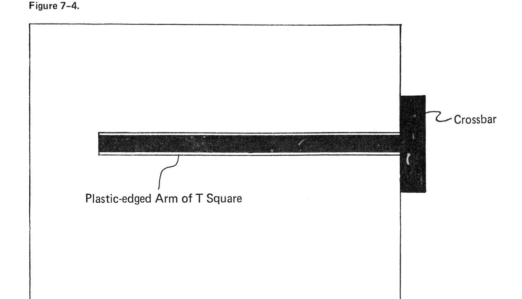

Crossbar

Plastic-edged Arm of T Square

To use a T square, employ the plastic edge as the guide for drawing horizontal lines. Place a ruler or architect's scale near the edge of the T square so that you can measure accurately lines that must be drawn a distinct length. Do not use the edge of the architect's scale to draw the lines. Architect's scales tend to get pretty banged up and bruised. Their edges are often rough and lines drawn with them are found to look disastrous! So unless you want your drawings to look like they've been through a war, depend upon the edge of the T square to guide your pencil. Therefore, use the architect's scale for the measurement and the plastic edge of the T-square arm as a guide in actually drawing the line.

Now try drawing that two-inch square again, using the T square. Do it this way: measure in, say, three inches from the edge of the paper, then begin to draw a line two inches long between the numbers "5" and "7" on the ruler, as shown in Figure 7-5.

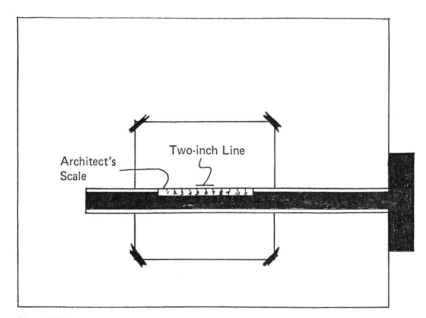

Figure 7-5.

Then move the T square two inches down from the line that you just drew and repeat the first step in drawing the second line. What now exists is a piece of paper with two two-inch-long parallel lines drawn five inches away from the edge of the paper (see Figure 7-6).

To finish the square, draw two vertical lines joining the ends of the horizontal lines. An easier way to do this part of the drawing will be shown soon, but for now it is acceptable to use the T square's edge. Figure 7-7 shows the finished product.

Now that you are an expert at using the T square, get another piece of scrap paper and draw another two-inch square. Time yourself again. It should take less time using the T square than it did to draw the first square. How did you do? Write down how long it took here: _____ . Worksheet 24 contains more practice exercises.

The T square is a very simple tool to use. Sometimes a drafting surface will be equipped with a *parallel bar*, which is used for the same purpose as the T square. The difference is that the p-bar is attached to the drafting surface permanently and may allow the designer

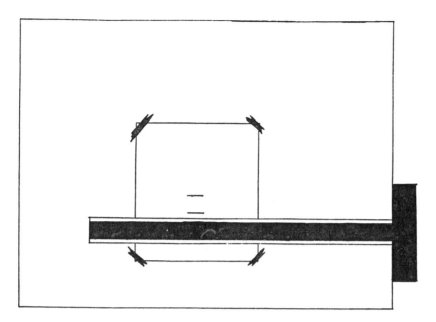

Figure 7–6.

Figure 7–7.

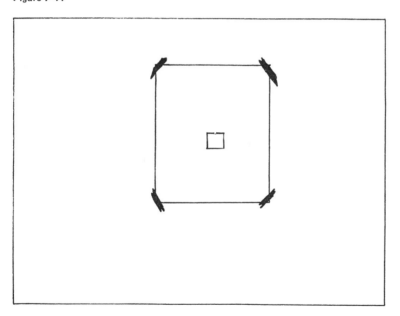

to be accurate without the care required to keep the T square properly in place on the work surface. The p-bar usually provides a quicker way to obtain satisfactory results. Like a T square, the p-bar slides up and down the work surface and provides the edge for horizontal line drawing. Obviously, if the drafting surface has a p-bar attached to it, you do not need a T square.

THE TRIANGLE

A triangle is a piece of clear plastic in the shape of a right triangle. You will use it in conjunction with the T square or parallel bar to draw vertical lines. Triangles come in various shapes and sizes, the most popular being the 30-60-90- and the 45-degree triangles. These two shapes are illustrated in Figure 7-8. We will discuss their different uses shortly. Right now, you probably want to know how to use a triangle to draw a vertical line. It's really *simple*—one of the easiest things you will do! Just place the triangle on the top edge of the T square or p-bar and use the perpendicular side of the triangle as the guide for the line (see Figure 7-9).

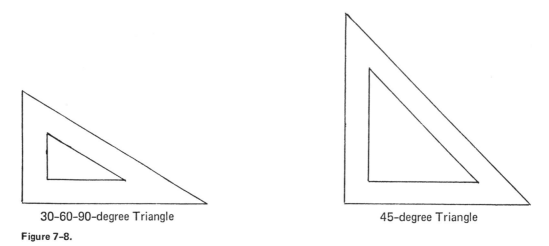

30–60–90-degree Triangle   45–degree Triangle

Figure 7–8.

Figure 7–9.

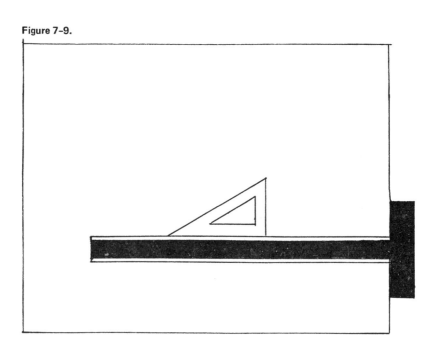

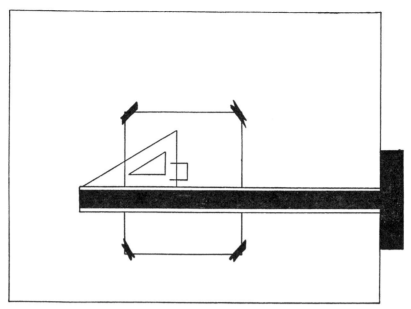

Figure 7-10.

Remember drawing the two-inch square with the T square? After drawing the two horizontal lines, you had to draw two vertical lines to complete the square. You had to improvise then, but no more! Now you are fully equipped to *architecturally draft* a square. Just use the triangle as instructed to add the vertical lines to the sketch. Slide the triangle along the straight edge to the appropriate place, as indicated in Figure 7-10.

See how much easier this way is than improvising with the T square? In case the competitive urge strikes, try drawing the two-inch square again and timing how long it takes. It should go quicker this time than ever before.

Why Are There Different Kinds of Triangles?

There are instances in drafting that suggest the use of a particular triangle, depending upon the angle of the line that you need to draw. Both the 30-60-90 triangle and the 45-degree triangle have 90-degree angles in them, so both may be used to draw perpendicular lines, as shown in Figure 7-9. Angles, though, are commonly required in architectural drafting, particularly to show symbols for doors and windows in floor plans. Chapter 9 includes illustrations of these architectural symbols. Take a look at them now to see why different triangles are useful.

Uniformity in drafting is a *must*. All angled lines symbolizing doors, windows, and the like *must* be the same. For instance, all doors with hinges, such as the front doors on most homes, must be drawn at the same angle from the wall. If each door symbol were different, the drawing would look sloppy and unprofessional, so since these design tools are available, take advantage of them. Oh, in the beginning they all may be a little hard to adjust to, but just give them a chance. Practice using them on Worksheets 25-28 and their beneficial aspects will become apparent.

CHAPTER EIGHT

LETTERING AND LABELING

Before you start to draft spaces for human needs, there is one more aspect of design we must explore, namely, the art and necessity of labeling all drawings. Why is labeling necessary? Because without any indication of what the drawing is, no one—professional or layperson—would be able to tell what has been done. They would have to rely upon a guess, which everyone in the design project wants to avoid like the plague. Any client looking at a project plan wants to know what he is looking at. He does not want to guess. Suppose that he misinterpreted ill-labeled plans. It would put the designer and her associates in an embarrassing position. This should not happen. When hired for a project, you must be professional at all times, and the visual work has to enhance your image as a respectable, dependable professional.

LETTERING

Let's look first at lettering. Remember, if possible, how it was back in first grade when you had a fat red pencil and wide-ruled paper to practice the alphabet on. Remember how academic your printing was then? So neat, according to the way the book said to do it. But what has happened since then? How is your printing now? Indeed, do you *ever* print anything? You just scribble, you say? What a bad habit to get into! If you are like most people, you probably resort to a mere facsimile of what was originally taught as handwriting. "Are we going to have to go back to first grade to learn to print?" you ask. No, that would be an insult at this point in life. No, it is not necessary to go back that far, at least not physically. Maybe mentally, though. Let's investigate for a minute. What is lettering anyway?

Can you tell a person's personality traits by examining handwriting? Supposedly characteristics such as friendliness, shrewdness, miserliness, security, insecurity, conformity, maverick tendencies, and intelligence, among others, are decipherable in a person's handwriting. A few other traits are also probably evident: creativity and conscientiousness, which happen to be two of the major concerns of this book. In this discussion these two words can be interpreted in this manner: creativity is the style of the lettering and conscientiousness relates to its neatness and overall presentation.

Once a designer has identified the problem, thought it through, and prepared some visuals to convey the solution, a method of identification for the visuals is necessary. Why not just record the information in normal, everyday handwriting? That would get the idea across, wouldn't it? No. In all likelihood, it would not look professional and would detract from the work.

Lettering, then, is the art of executing an easily readable, attractive, and perhaps unique and distinctive—but at least uniform and legible—form of writing to explain project

Figure 8-1.

visuals. Uniformity is very important here. Uniform lettering can convey a feeling of dependability, which clients greatly desire.

Different types of lettering elicit different emotional reactions, as illustrated in Figure 8-1. Do the words seem to coincide with the style of lettering used to express them? (Turn to Worksheet 29.)

There are many ways of writing, and we all quite naturally write differently. Our handwriting is an expression of who we are. Lettering should be, too. The goal is to develop a personal style that is neat, readable, and attractive. It should be also relatively easy to do. There is not a bit of sense in adopting a difficult style for constant use. Choose a simple style that you can do proficiently. It's like diving: a dive with a high degree of difficulty can really put you on top if it is done well, but the consequences if it is missed can be unpleasant. It's all right to try the difficult occasionally, but for general usage, select a type of lettering with a lower degree of difficulty.

The first thing to do is to try your hand (pun entirely intended) at some different types of lettering. Start with some simple types, like those on Worksheets 30–32. Make the letters as much like the original "guide letters" as possible. Additional practice on graph paper is advisable. After that, use the graph paper more creatively. Using the lines as guides, change the character of the letters by changing their size and shape. Practicing lettering is the only way to become proficient and comfortable with it. So *practice a lot*! And don't forget to practice numbers, too.

LABELING

Lettering, of course, identifies what has been done. On a drawing, all major areas of the designed space should be labeled, and the name of that entire space, which may be the title of the entire project, must also be noted. The name goes in a title block, which is a section of the presentation board or paper that is blocked off. The title block contains the designer's name, the date, the project title, and other details necessary to describe the project.

Look at the drawing in Figure 8-2 and try to tell what type of space it is. What is it? Are you at a loss for words? What do you *think* it is? Is just *thinking* good enough? Guessing, as mentioned earlier, is *not* good enough. Kick yourself if you answered "yes" to that question. Never leave anything to chance. Don't allow anything to be misunderstood. Again, neglecting to clarify yourself can give your client a poor impression of you as a professional. Be as explicit as possible.

When labeling a drawing, you should make all lettering the best you have to offer. Make it clear and attractive so that it will enhance the drawing. Compare the two drawings in Figure 8-3. Quite a difference, isn't there? Looking at the drawings and assuming that two different people drew them, which one would you hire for the big, important, multimillion-dollar job? Why? Always remember that first impressions are critical. Think back to Chapter 4 and how human behavior influences people. The first impression a person gives when applying for a job or presenting a solution, in all likelihood, will be a lasting one. In the design and housing professions you must take it upon yourself to make sure you make the most favorable impression possible.

One thing is extremely important here. There will be many times when a prospective employer will not see *you*, the designer, and your work has to do the talking for you. In such cases, it is necessary to be quite sure that your work is the best that it can be. A lot—perhaps a career—depends upon it!

Worksheet 33 has a labeling problem for you.

DIMENSIONING

In addition to the need to name the spaces that you have planned, design projects require another form of description. Look again at Figure 8-3 and try to guess what else would be helpful in determining more about the drawing. Is there anything else that the drawing is not telling about the space? In case this question is causing trouble, here is a hint: how large is the bathroom? It doesn't say, does it? Therein lies the answer: Figure 8-3 gives no clue as to the sizes of any of the spaces.

Numbers and lines that appear on sketches are called *dimensions* and *dimensioning*, respectively. This section describes the process of drawing in dimension lines and adding

Figure 8-2.

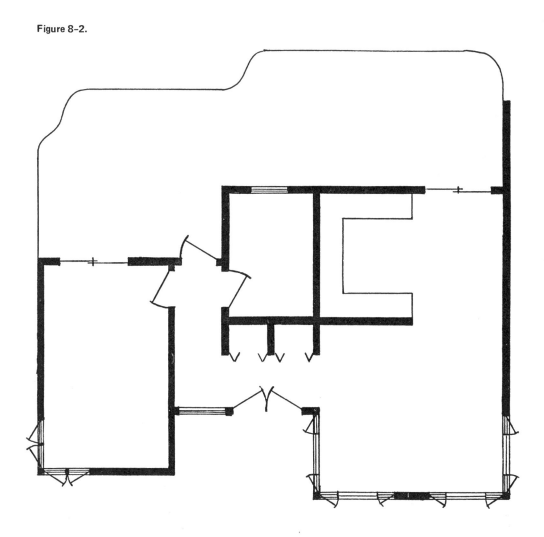

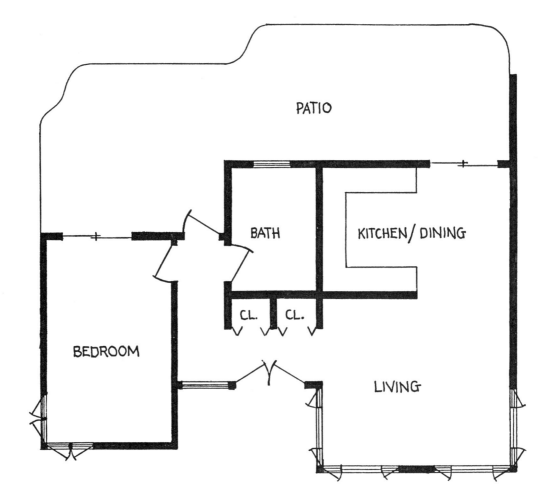

Figure 8–3a.

Figure 8–3b.

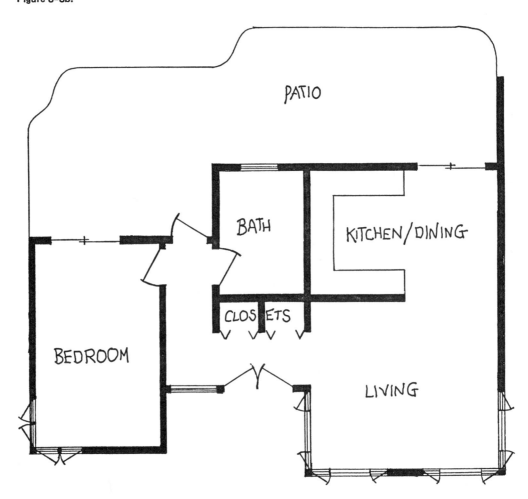

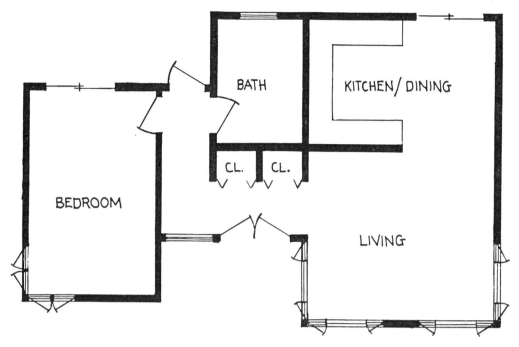

Figure 8-4.

the appropriate measurements for every wall, window, and door. And that means *every*. Do not leave *anything* undimensioned. Look at Figure 8-4 to see how to do it.

All dimension lines should be the exact length of the object they describe. Arrows at each end of the line further clarify what the measurements refer to. Leaving a break in the dimension line in which to insert the dimension itself, as illustrated, seems to be the least confusing method for including the necessary numbers. There are alternatives, such as putting the dimensions just above the accompanying dimension line, but when many dimensions are required, other systems could be more than a little confusing. Look again at Figure 8-4 to see how a dimensioned drawing looks. Study it thoroughly. Now turn to Worksheet 34 and try it yourself. In order to make the drawing neat, keep as many dimension lines as possible a uniform distance from the objects they are measuring and from each other (see Figure 8-4).

There is one way to cheat, so to speak, and show sizes on the drawing without using dimensions. Just write the scale near the drawing. That way, anyone looking at it will have at least a rough idea of measurements and with an architect's scale, can figure out the precise dimensions. This technique is particularly useful for the presentation of an accurately drawn space without cluttering up the drawing with all of its dimensions. Sometimes dimensioning a drawing fully is not desirable, so in case someone accuses you of taking the lazy way out because you did not include all of the dimensions, fight back! It is perfectly acceptable.

Labeling and dimensioning are two aspects of drafting that you must practice and master in order to produce adequate drawings. Poor lettering can ruin a perfect drawing.

Be sure to keep your work neat at all times. This principle cannot be stressed enough. One slip-up on dimensioning, for example, could prove fatal. A drawing that is mislabeled or misdimensioned or lettering that is indecipherable could bring big trouble. Did you ever wonder how a pharmacist feels when trying to figure out just what a particular doctor has prescribed for a patient? Doctors are notorious for their handwriting, and just because you *know* that pharmacists *must* have a course entitled "Basic Chirography Deciphering 101," you cannot assume that the general public also takes such a class. Be neat! It will help more than you realize. Think neat as you prepare the assignment on Worksheet 35. Do it now.

ALTERNATIVES TO HANDWRITTEN LETTERING

There are a few alternatives to lettering should dissatisfaction with your own effort occur or if a special effect is desirable. Various styles of press-on lettering (see Figure 9-1) are available in art supply stores. Sheets of preprinted lettering mean all the user has to do is transfer the desired letters to the paper or board with direct pressure.

One major disadvantage of press-on lettering is its cost. It is relatively expensive and must be purchased often as it is not reusable. Also, since it comes on transfer sheets, it may chip off when it is handled.

Stenciling is another alternative. A stencil is a much more permanent and durable investment than press-on lettering since it can be used and reused indefinitely, or until it either wears out or breaks.

Press-on lettering is generally more stylish, so if a unique effect is desirable, you may want to use it. For general use, however, a stencil or your own personal method is perhaps the best alternative.

SUMMARY

Up to this point, we have looked at human behavior and its relationships to spatial layout. Space and values depend upon creativity for their development and upon methodology for their organization. Now you have some of the skills necessary to visually present design ideas initiated in Unit 1 of this book. The three chapters in this section provide *basic* knowledge for recording plans, but remember that what you have learned is only a beginning. There are many visual and drafting aids yet to discover and investigate. New products become available all the time. So, use your new skills to propel you into the next section, where you will learn drawing that will be indispensable.

One more thing: if at any point you should wonder how in the world a specific space came to be designed and drawn, go back and read through Chapters 3 and 4. They should provide reassuring "reasons-for-doing." In any conscientiously designed plan, the subjects discussed in the first four chapters of this book were carefully investigated and utilized.

UNIT THREE

IDEA
REPRESENTATION

OBJECTIVES

Upon completion of this unit, you should be able to:

1. Incorporate the design concepts of creativity, space, and values methodologically into physical spaces appropriate for human use.
2. Represent a design solution utilizing the four different illustration techniques presented in this unit: floor plan, elevation, one-, and two-point perspective.
3. Construct a model of a design solution.

How often have you heard it said that "A picture is worth a thousand words"? Do you think it's true? If you don't, you may be in for a little trouble about now because this section of the book deals with the development of the visuals needed to express your version of a design solution. Its basic premise lies in the belief that "pictures" are the most indispensable aspect of a design presentation, primarily because they show what the design solution will look like. Your clients will not have to imagine to any great extent how you are planning to spend their money.

It is very important to remember this: you are being trained to think visually. If someplace or something is described to you, you should be able to imagine it fairly well, provided the verbal description is accurate and complete. In addition, you should be able to picture space reasonably well—length, width, depth, and height. However, most of your clients will not have these capabilities, and it would be inconsiderate of you to think that they should. Remember, just as you would be at a loss were someone to ask you to perform open-heart surgery, others are equally at a loss to interpret design specifications and drawings. Both are complex, demanding, exacting, and require specialized instruction to master.

Five major types of design illustration will be introduced here. Since the floor is the most influential part of a space, floor plans will be the first topic, followed by elevations, which are drawings that illustrate wall detail. Following that chapter, model building, which involves an elevation of each wall and a floor plan, is a logical next step. As you will see, model building is fairly easy, although it is time-consuming. But it is also a lot of fun. Most important, it permits the designer to illustrate a design solution in three dimensions, something that is very helpful to both designer and client because it greatly reduces the necessity for imagination on the part of the client. In a scale model of the design solution, nothing is drastically misrepresented.

Perspective drawing follows that. One- and two-point perspectives, the most useful renderings to express design ideas, are also a necessary part of your illustration arsenal, and in Chapters 12–14, you will learn simple methods for drawing them. The methods are not "architectural" in heritage; they are designed so that you will be able to free-hand sketch perspectives shortly, if you practice.

A problem that occurs often in the interior design and housing fields is one that, in fact, has created itself. Those people who are unfamiliar with the fields place undue emphasis upon visuals, believing them to be an end unto themselves—sort of like being both the parent and the child together. "Not so!" you should be interjecting at this point. It is of the utmost importance to impart the fact that these visuals have been created as a result of a study of the human values and needs that determine spatial design: human behavior. These aspects of design, treated both creatively and methodologically, give birth and life to a problem. Only after a designer has completely analyzed them can he or she synthesize an appropriate solution.

So do not forget the design theory you learned earlier in this book. Without the prerequisite study of human behavior, these drawings would be inappropriate, if not impossible, because the solutions they would represent would not derive logically from the problem's analysis. They would represent the wrapping paper that is totally unrelated to the present's contents.

Just keep this in mind as you read the following chapters. There will be references back to the chapters on space, values, and creativity, and you will be asked to design spaces according to the ideas presented in them.

CHAPTER NINE

FLOOR PLAN DRAWING

The floor is the most important part of a space. Without a floor it would be rather difficult, if not downright dangerous, to enter a space. Besides giving firm footing, it provides places for you to put things. Furniture, carpeting, lamps, people—they all have something to relate to if a floor is present. If it were not there, everything would fall into a no-person's land, somewhere beneath their intended spot, to be discovered at some future time by archaeologists trying to see how we lived 'way back "now."

Floors are horizontal surfaces. They have measurements in two dimensions: length and width. When assigned to draw the floor plan of a space, get a tape measure or a ruler of some sort, and measure the floor completely. (It is helpful to remember that in design you should hurry up and be successful so that you can afford to have an assistant crawl around on the floor to do the measuring and a draftsman to do all of the drafting. That way, you can concentrate your energy on the more vital aspects of life.)

Human behavior at least influences and *ideally* should *control* physical spatial delineation. Often this is not the case due to such external constraints as cost and existing architectural features. It is quite apparent that the specific activities that a space is to support will determine the furnishings that will be placed in it. For example, in a room that will be used as a dirty space for a ceramicist, an antique dining table and chairs to be used for formal meals would seem quite outrageous to most people.

Area size is also subject to the intended purpose. The activities that are to be performed in a space indicate what objects should be included there. The area must accommodate the sizes and shapes of these objects. In addition, human beings require a minimum amount of space for easy passage through and usage of an area. All of these measurements combine to suggest basic room sizes.

Figure 9-1 illustrates the conditions that help determine spatial configurations. They range from the tangible (furniture sizes and shapes, clearances, open space, area size, area shape) to the intangible (human behavior, activities). It shows the interrelationships among

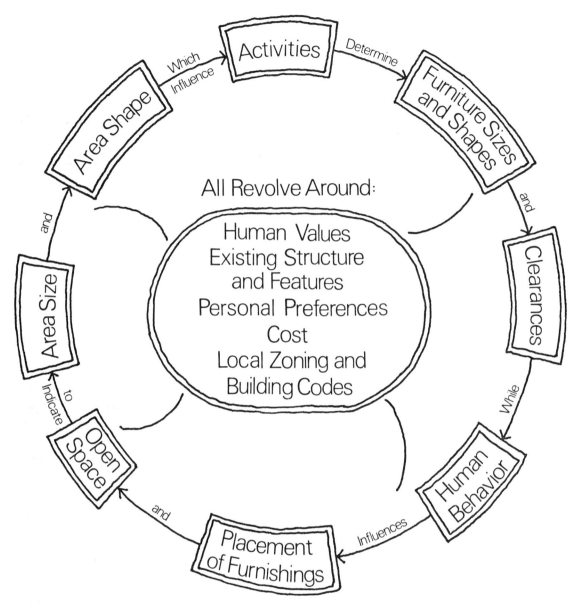

Figure 9-1.

all of these and also indicates their dependence upon human values, existing structures and features, personal preferences, cost, local zoning laws, and building codes.

Except for built-in furnishings, allow one or two inches of space between all objects and the wall. The recommended amount of space for a walkway between objects is at least two feet. Three feet is better. To understand why, stand perfectly still, one side against a wall, and measure how wide you are. This dimension is the minimum clearance, or distance, for passage, that you should plan for. Now have a friend help you determine how much space you need to walk normally. This measurement will be greater than when you stood still and will give you a good idea of how much clearance to allow.

Figure 9-2.

Does all of this sound familiar? It should. What you just did was to measure yourself anthropometrically. Yes, anthropometrics has been lurking in a dark closet all this time, just waiting to haunt you (Figure 9-2).

It is rather difficult, and indeed a poor practice, to name distinct room sizes. Do all room uses dictate a rectangular or square shape? These are the shapes usually conjured up by contractors. Cost-wise, they are the most economical, but use-wise, they often are bland.

People are attracted to little alcoves and other out-of-the-way extraordinary spaces that older homes often have. People usually devise uses for spaces like that before they work out what to do with the main part of the area.

These are some of the principles that you should keep in mind when you decide on room size. Do not lock yourself into a specific area shape. Follow the advice of Figure 9-1 in determining spaces.

As mentioned earlier, square and rectangular shapes are the most economical to construct, and because costs place housing out of the reach of so many people today, economy is important, although not at the expense of ingenious, creative design. Even a "box" can be quite unique, as the spatial delineation in Figure 8-5 shows.

Well, then, what is the *ideal* way to design a specific space? Before revealing that secret, why do people in interior design and housing, as well as others in creative vocations, start with the ideal? Think back to the discussion on creativity in Chapter 2. Specifically, recall the word "imagineering": let your imagination soar first, then engineer it back to reality. It is easier to think wildly first, without imposing restrictions upon yourself, than to form your solution with, say, constant knowledge of the shape of the space in mind.

Figure 9-3.

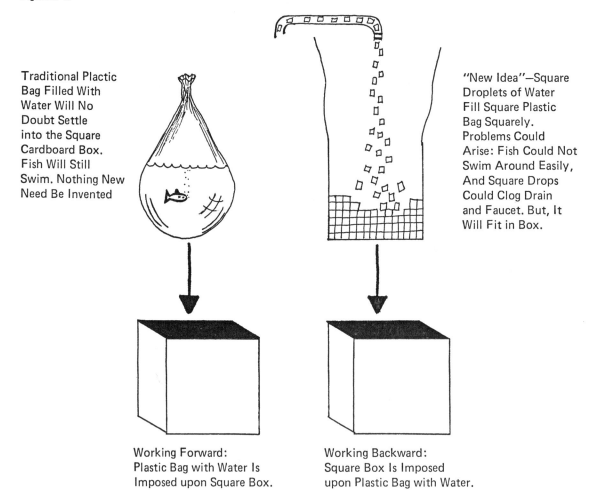

Traditional Plastic Bag Filled With Water Will No Doubt Settle into the Square Cardboard Box. Fish Will Still Swim. Nothing New Need Be Invented

"New Idea"—Square Droplets of Water Fill Square Plastic Bag Squarely. Problems Could Arise: Fish Could Not Swim Around Easily, And Square Drops Could Clog Drain and Faucet. But, It Will Fit in Box.

Working Forward: Plastic Bag with Water Is Imposed upon Square Box.

Working Backward: Square Box Is Imposed upon Plastic Bag with Water.

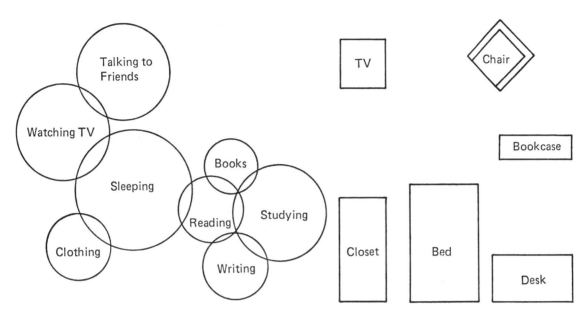

Figure 9-4.

Think about a plastic bag filled with water. When you squeeze the open end together with your hand and hold it high, the water and bag form a huge droplike shape. For easy and safe transportation, you put the bag in a square cardboard box, and the bag of water conforms to the square shape. Figure 9-3 illustrates how versatile the bag of water is and how it, the *ideal* material, can be "engineered" back to reality with a square cardboard box,

Figure 9-5.

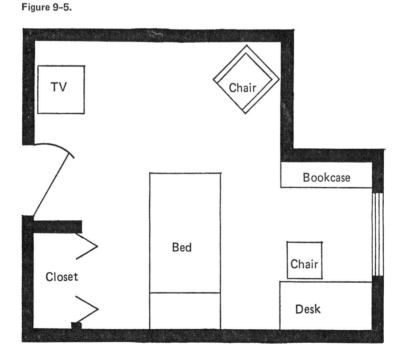

which is a constraint. Imagine the design problems that would occur in the production of a round cardboard box. Or a drop-shaped one. We might look at the problem from the other direction, though. Suppose you gave a square cardboard box to someone who knew little about water or plastic and told him that a plastic bag of water had to fit into the box. "There are two requirements here," say you, the designer. "First, the plastic bag must form a square shape when it is filled, and second, in order to meet the first requirement correctly, water must be made to 'drop' in little square shapes, much the way salt comes out of a salt shaker. That way we can be sure that this bag of water will fit into this square box." Do you see the point? Keeping the constraints in mind can affect creativity and, as shown here, the ability to reason. Do it the other way!

Returning now to the idea of how to ideally design space, we can begin by utilizing a schematic drawing to organize the activities that have been given. The activities, remember, suggest the furnishings, and the bubble diagram shown in Figure 9-4 might generate the accompanying drawing of objects. From this stage a general room size and shape will result, as shown in Figure 9-5. Furniture placement will also dictate locations of doors and windows, which should be drawn at this time, as shown in Figure 9-5.

This is, by necessity, a very amorphous method for determining the size and shape of a space. The idea is to retain an open mind: be a "glass box" instead of a "black box," in other words. Let the design evolve. Don't force it, and you will have a better chance of success. Now let your imagination soar to complete Worksheets 36 and 37.

What follows now is a step-by-step description of how to draw a floor plan. Some important "whys" are included, too. There are two ways to begin this sequence. One is to create a space on your own and just begin drawing it, and the other is to start with an existing space. The procedure is identical for both situations, with the exception of the first two steps. For a newly created space, begin by making a rough sketch of what is desired, as shown in Figure 9-6. Just draw whatever shape the identified needs warrant. Next, *select* the sizes that you desire. Since this is a theoretical place for now, there are no

Figure 9-6.

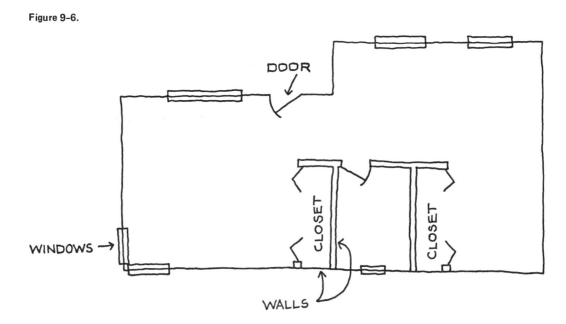

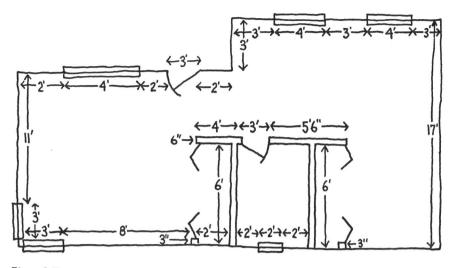

Figure 9-7.

real environmental constraints on your work. Measurements for the hypothetical space are shown in Figure 9-7.

When drawing an existing space, you begin in a slightly different manner. The best way to begin drawing a floor plan is to make a rough sketch of that space as it appears. It is not necessary that this sketch be in any way accurate dimensionally, as long as it includes all of the architectural features that are present. It might look like the sketch in Figure 9-6, which shows the closets, doorways, windows, and walls along with the general shape of the space. Keep in mind that although this sketch does not have to be accurate with regard to its measurements, it must be neat and include all information that you will need to refer to later.

Second, measure the existing space accurately and completely, and add those measurements to the sketch, as illustrated in Figure 9-7. Be sure to measure *everything;* check and double-check your measurements. At this point, the drawing will resemble Figure 9-7. Make sure that all of the measurements total properly: the total measurements from opposite walls must equal each other (east equals west, north equals south).

This sketch will now contain a lot of information and you very easily might have created a colossal mess! But don't do that! You have to be neat, because it has been proven conclusively that the messier the sketch is, the greater the chance of making a mistake, which you must avoid at all costs. Of course, if you want to make mistakes, you know a good way to begin.

Be extra careful in recording measurements on the sketch. Use arrows that are long enough to show what a measurement refers to, and be sure that the accompanying figures are accurate. One slip-up could be disastrous! Extra care now will prevent embarrassing and time-consuming moments later. Remember, dumb mistakes can be costly, and none of us ever outgrows falling prey to them. But, being conscientious at all times can lessen their occurrence.

After you have completed the rough preliminary sketch, measured the space, and verified that the measurements are absolutely perfect, you are in business—almost. Now collect all the equipment you need to draw a floor plan. This work requires a work surface of some type—preferably a slant-top drafting table—and a seat—preferably one with a back so that it will support *your* back and you will be comfortable and able to work longer in one position. Then find an architect's scale, pencils, an eraser, a triangle, a compass, and a T square (if the work surface has a parallel bar, you will not need a T square). Last, find some paper and masking tape to adhere the paper to the work surface. *Now* you really are ready to begin.

First, using a small piece of masking tape at each corner of the paper, anchor the paper to the work surface. This step will save time and needless mistakes caused by floating paper. Check to see that the bottom edge of the paper is parallel to the bottom edge of the work surface. The drawing will look better on the paper if it is square in relation to the sheet's borders.

When drawing, always use a straight edge of some sort, preferably a triangle and the parallel bar or the T square. The edge of an architect's scale often gets battered, remember, and so the lines you draw with it might not be as accurate as they should be.

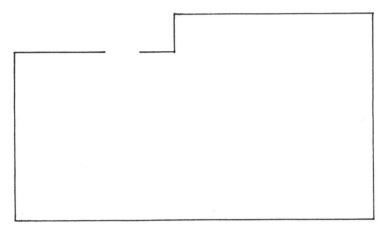

Figure 9-8.

Figure 9-9.

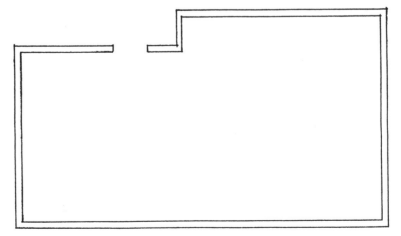

After selecting the drawing instruments and materials, take a look at the sketch that you made of the space. Begin drawing it by first outlining the outside walls as shown in Figure 9-8. Now check the drawing's measurements against the ones on the preliminary sketch. If they are incorrect, fix them! Next, put in the wall thicknesses on the "outside" of the space. Marking the wall thicknesses within the existing lines will reduce the size of the space and cause the drawing to become too small. Your drawing should resemble Figure 9-9. The scale of Figure 9-9 is one-eighth inch. Measure it with your architect's scale, and you will see that it is quite a large space. Imagine that it is a living space for one person. We must now make some decisions as to how to divide the area. Analyzing the purposes for its existence is, of course, a major part of the space's development. It is, after all, the way to learn the space's function. After having analyzed the space as described in the first part of this book, you can draw actual physical limitations, such as walls, floors, doors, and windows. Let's say that we have already done this much, so we know where the walls will be. The result of architecturally drafting them and their thicknesses in the space is shown in Figure 9-10.

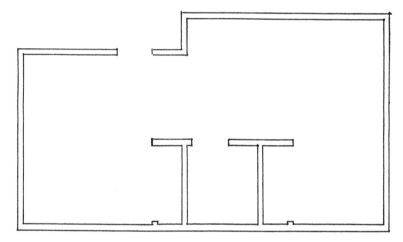

Figure 9-10.

Doors and windows follow. One of the purposes of producing a drawing of a space is to illustrate it simply, without a verbal explanation. To that end, symbols are very useful. Figure 9-11 illustrates some of the more common door and window types and their corresponding symbols; learn them well. Figure 9-12 shows what this particular space looks like when the doors and windows are properly added to the drawing. (Complete Worksheets 38 and 39.)

Again, the selection and placement of these architectural features does not occur randomly. For instance, psychologically speaking, people *need* sunlight. This requirement and other, more purely utilitarian and aesthetically determined preferences dictate window placement. Proper window placement can eliminate the need for excessive artificial lighting. It can provide welcome, natural scenic relief in a potentially drab, sterile environment. In other words, it can be both psychologically and physically rewarding. Window placement, therefore, is the result of *careful selection. It doesn't just happen!*

Figure 9–11.

(a) Door and Doorway Symbols—For use on floorplans and elevations. The symbol on top represents how the door or doorway would be drawn in an elevation; the symbol on the bottom represents how the door or doorway would be drawn on a floorplan.

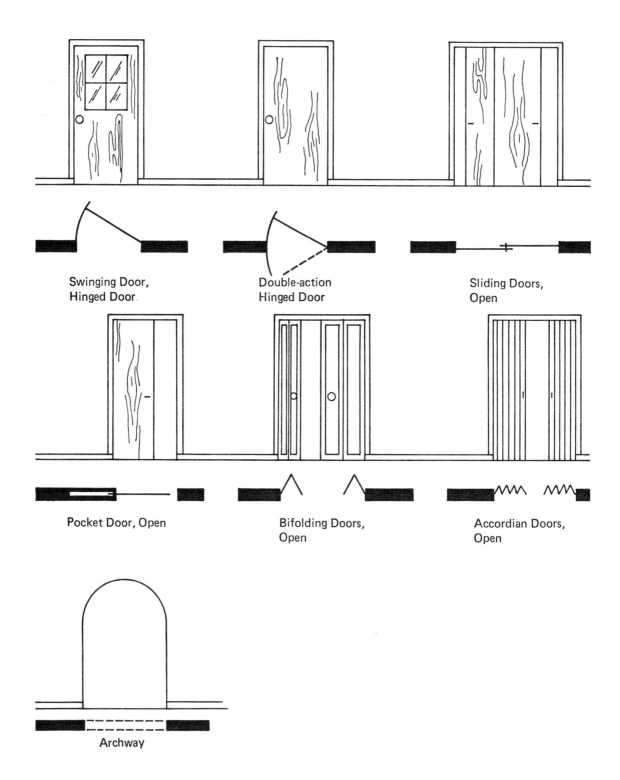

Swinging Door,
Hinged Door.

Double-action
Hinged Door

Sliding Doors,
Open

Pocket Door, Open

Bifolding Doors,
Open

Accordian Doors,
Open

Archway

Figure 9–11 continued.

(b) Window Symbols—For use on floor plans and elevations. The symbol on top represents how the window would be drawn in an elevation; the symbol on the bottom represents how the window would be drawn on a floor plan.

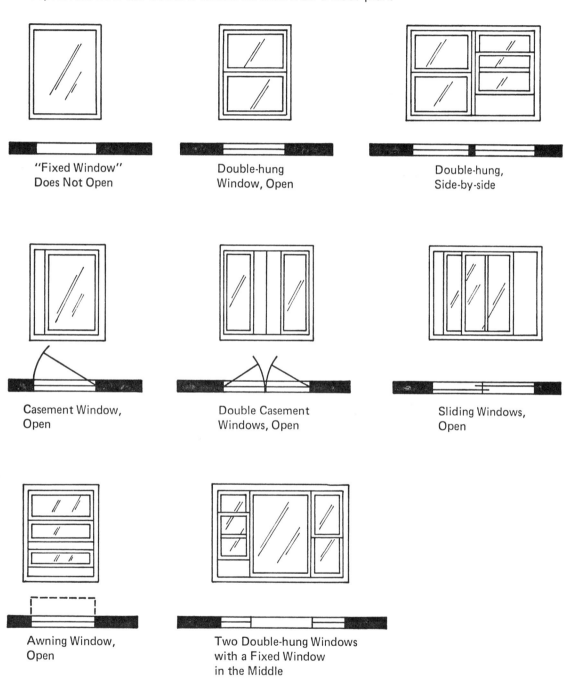

"Fixed Window"
Does Not Open

Double-hung
Window, Open

Double-hung,
Side-by-side

Casement Window,
Open

Double Casement
Windows, Open

Sliding Windows,
Open

Awning Window,
Open

Two Double-hung Windows
with a Fixed Window
in the Middle

Figure 9-11 continued.

(c) Stairway Symbols—For use on floor plans and elevations.
The symbol on top represents how the stairway would be
drawn in an elevation; the symbol on the bottom represents
how the stairway would be drawn on a floorplan.

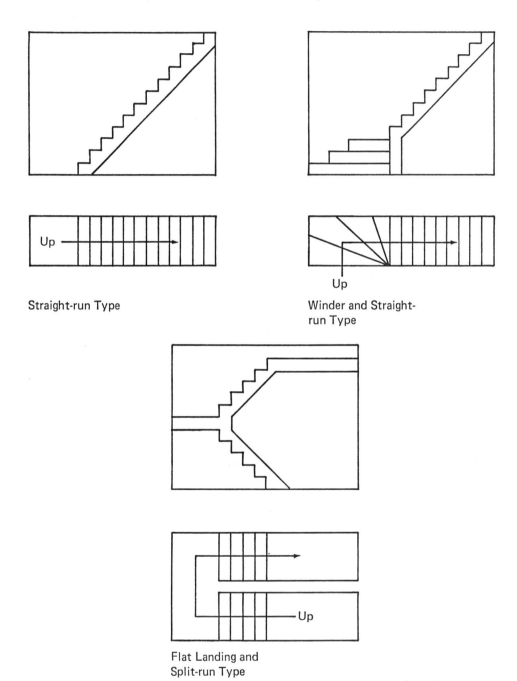

Straight-run Type

Winder and Straight-
run Type

Flat Landing and
Split-run Type

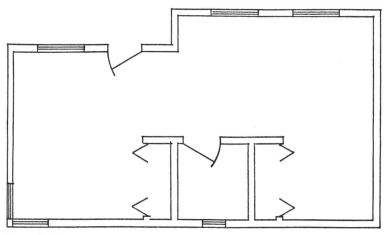

Figure 9-12.

Door selection and placement also depend upon human needs and preferences. How many doors are necessary? What kind? Human values provide reasons for such things as doors: privacy gives a good reason for having a front door and also for having doors on bedrooms to isolate them from the rest of the home. Wanting to hide our untidy habits, if, indeed, any of us have them, is a terrific reason for putting doors on closets and on the

Figure 9-13.

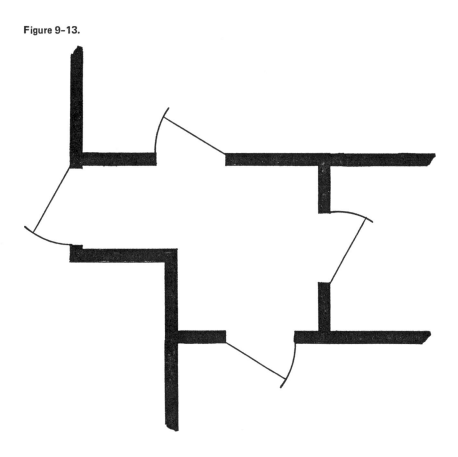

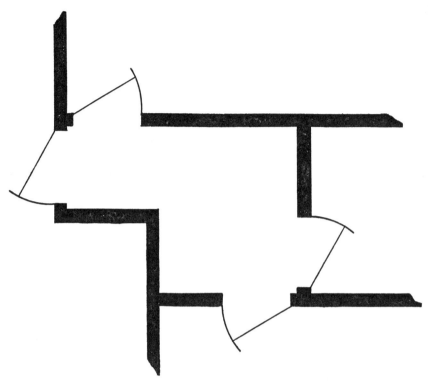

Figure 9-14.

room that we seem to use for everything messy and that we really want to hide. The traffic pattern in a space will suggest appropriate door positions. Consider Figure 9-13. Here is a space with so many doorways that any type of efficient spatial usage is nearly impossible. Furniture placement is possible only if the pieces are small, and even they might impede traffic through the space. In fact, this space has become a large hallway, hasn't it? Take out

Figure 9-15.

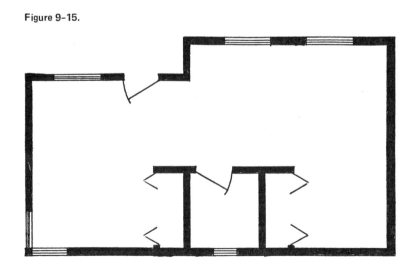

a piece of scratch paper and see if you can improve this poor space's plight. A possible solution is shown in Figure 9-14.

Getting back to the drawing, it is necessary to make it easier to read than Figure 9-12. Darkening the walls is a good visual aid, as Figure 9-15 shows. Figures 9-12 and 9-15 are the same drawing, but Figure 9-15 makes better visual sense.

The basic drawing is now finished. The door and wall symbols are big helps because they explain without words what the various openings in the walls are. Just looking at the standardized symbol tells us whether the door is a swinging one, a bifolding one, or an accordion type. The same is true of windows. At a glance it is apparent that they are double-hung, casement, awning, or other type. Learn these symbols and use them. See Figure 9-11.

Right now, take another look at Figure 9-15. If this is a living space for one person, where is the kitchen? The bathroom? Eating space? Aha! So we're back to the old labeling game again. Labeling it even as simply as in Figure 9-16 helps.

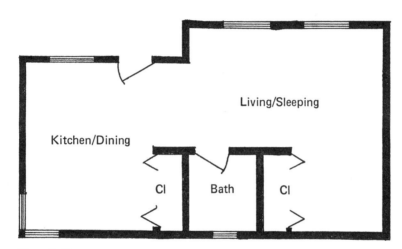

Figure 9-16.

Figure 9-17.

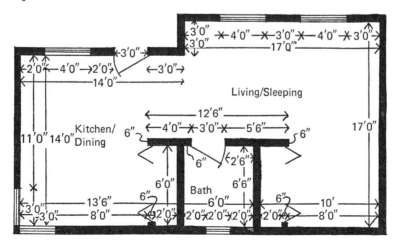

Remember, in Chapter 8 ("Lettering and Labeling") you read that dimensioning is a form of labeling that provides a great deal of insight (see Figure 9-17). There is another type of labeling—loosely interpreted. Harking back to the idea of object representation through symbols, we must add furnishings to the drawing. Line drawings that show the outer shape of the object are most common. Added details, such as fabric patterns, upholstery, and wood grain, appear occasionally, but generally do not. Figure 9-18 shows how the same drawing might look with this type of "labeling."

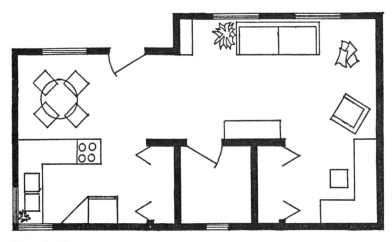

Figure 9-18.

Deciding which style to use to detail a drawing will depend upon the nature of the problem. For some problems, a very general type of label like the style of Figure 9-15 is desirable. Remember to include the "scale" in this case to permit determination of area sizes by the viewer. For projects requiring greater detail, one of the methods shown in Figures 9-17 and 9-18 is recommended. Again, the intent will dictate what technique is best.

Above all else, always keep the drawings neat. This is especially necessary in floor-plan drawing because one seemingly minor misrepresentation could distort the entire plan. Floor plans serve as guides for builders and any mistakes may result in construction problems.

The task analysis and task description, respectively, answer the questions "What will I draw?" and "How will I draw it?" Therefore the next section details the necessary steps to follow when drawing a floor plan. Use them in doing Worksheets 40 and 41.

TASK DESCRIPTION AND TASK ANALYSIS

Task Description

Given all of the necessary architectural drawing equipment, you will be able to represent a given space as a floor plan drawing on tracing vellum in half- or quarter-inch scale.

Task Analysis

21 steps

1. Collect a tape measure, pencil, and paper and go to the space to be drawn, or select a room from the house floor plan that appears in this chapter.
2. Sketch a preliminary drawing of that space.
3. Measure and record, in pencil, all room measurements on the preliminary sketch so that the actual wall measurements correspond to the appropriate lines on the sketch.
4. Verify all measurements by adding together the total width of the south wall and comparing the result to the total width of the north wall. Then compare the total length of the east wall to the total length of the west wall.
5. If all the measurements check out, then go on to the next step. If they do not, then go back to step 3.
6. Assemble all needed equipment (triangle, T square—if necessary—architect's scale, small-size tracing vellum, masking tape, pencils, eraser, compass) on an appropriate drafting surface.
7. Place the tracing vellum on the drafting surface. Be sure to position the bottom of the vellum parallel to the bottom of the drafting surface.
8. Tape the tracing vellum to the drafting surface with masking tape by placing a small piece of tape at each corner.
9. If you have correctly taped the tracing vellum to the drafting surface, that is, if the bottom edge of the paper is parallel to the bottom edge of the drafting surface, then go on to the next step. If it is not, then go back to step 7, replace the vellum and retape it.
10. Draw the outside walls of the space in scale.
11. Draw the outer-wall thicknesses of the space in scale.
12. Check to see that the measurements on the drawing coincide with those taken from the room. If they do, proceed to the next step. If not, go back to step 3 and verify your measurements again.
13. Draw the inner walls and thicknesses in the space in scale.
14. Check to see that the inner-wall measurements on the drawing coincide with those taken from the room. If they don't, go back to step 3. Verify the measurements again. When the measurements are correct, go on to the next step.
15. Draw all door and window symbols in scale.
16. Draw all built-in and freestanding furniture in scale.
17. Verify all measurements on the finished drawing to make sure they correspond exactly with those taken from the room and recorded on the preliminary sketch. If they don't, go back to step 3 and verify the measurements.
18. Label the finished drawing according to the needs that you have established. The labeling can take the form of dimensioning, as shown in Figure 9-16; area labeling, as shown in Figure 9-16; or furnishing drawing, as indicated in Figure 9-18.
19. Supply all information requested in the title block.
20. Look back over the drawing and be sure that you have properly shown everything.
21. Hand the completed drawing to the instructor on the date assigned.

FLOOR PLANS: ANOTHER DIMENSION

Before allocating floor plans strictly to the "architectural drafting only" box, we must take note of the fact that these drawings can also be a valuable tool for conveying color, texture, materials, and furnishings. By eliminating all dimensioning and labeling that uses words and either drawing the floor plan on a heavy board or adhering the paper on which the drawing appears to a board, you can easily transform it into a visual that people who are unfamiliar with design visuals will appreciate.

After carefully measuring, recording, and drawing the space, add color and detail to it. For example, if you have used carpeting on the floor, illustrate it with color and texture. You can show wood flooring with wood grain and wood color. Furniture should have detail, too. Imagine yourself hovering directly above a chair, table, or sofa. Draw what you would see. Don't indicate merely the outer edges of the furniture as you have done before: show the arms, back, color, and texture of the piece. A drawing like this one must be architecturally correct, but it should also present the space as a "comfortable" place to be. This type of floor plan can be a very pleasing design visual, as well as being easy to understand.

Keep in mind, though, that an elaborate floor plan will not eliminate the need for the more "architectural" floor plan. This floor plan will be an addition to that plan. The architectural floor plan is essential to your design solution presentation. The new version is optional. Figure 9-18 illustrates this technique to a minimal degree. To produce a truly artistic drawing you would have to fill in more details.

Now create a fancy floor plan. The task description and task analysis that follow will guide you through this exercise.

TASK DESCRIPTION AND TASK ANALYSIS II

Task Description

Given all of the necessary architectural drawing equipment, you will be able to represent a given space as a detailed, artistic drawing. Do the drawing in quarter- or half-inch scale on or adhere it to illustration board.

Task Analysis

21 steps

1. Follow the preceding task analysis through step 16, but substitute illustration board or a good-quality white paper for the tracing vellum in step 5.
17. Darken the walls with black or brown ink.
18. Add artistic detail to the plan: color, texture, shadows, "comfort." Make the details distinct enough to be visible from a distance of about ten feet.

19. If you have drawn this visual on paper, *carefully and accurately* cut around the wall edges and adhere the drawing to the illustration board with paper cement. The drawing should look as if it was drawn directly on the illustration board.
20. Supply all information requested in the title block.
21. Hand the completed drawing to the instructor on the date assigned.

CHAPTER TEN

ELEVATION DRAWING

Floor plans are really great drawings to have around. They are most beneficial in illustrating the length and width of spaces, including wall and door types and their placement. If someone were to say that all a contractor needs as a reference to build a particular space is a floor plan, would you agree? Rather than list all of the reasons why it would be totally, absurdly wrong to believe that statement, we will examine here the virtues of the elevation.

Elevations, a second component of design visuals, reveal aspects of spaces that floor plans do not. Elevations are detailed drawings of walls: they show height. They indicate

Figure 10-1.

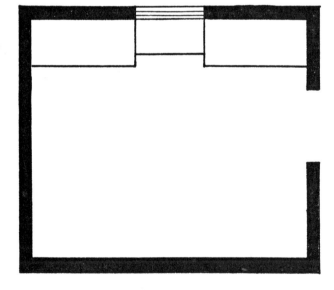

ceiling height, the placement of furniture and accessories on walls, and wall finishings, among other details appropriate for a particular space. When a person sees an elevation, he should be able to decipher what materials are being used where, and this goal is accomplished, again, through the use of symbols. Some symbols appear in the illustrations in this chapter and in Figure 9-11, but many of them are left to the illustrator's imagination. Anything that will represent the actual material is acceptable. Right now, let's take a look at how an elevation differs from a floor plan.

An elevation complements a floor plan, and vice versa. Looking at Figure 10-1, you can see that the corresponding elevation drawing fills in a lot of details that the floor plan only suggests. For instance, the floor plan says that there are two "chests" and a "seat" on the wall, as well as a double-hung window. But is it possible to tell from the floor plan what kind of window treatment has been used? Or how tall the chests are? What about the seat— what style is it? Does it have a cushion? Going back to the window, how tall is it and how much wall space is below it? Ah, the disadvantages of a floor plan. These drawings say a lot, but not enough. The elevation answers all of our questions. Taking another look at Figure 10-1, can you understand its value?

One thing that a floor plan shows that an elevation does not is *depth*. It is impossible to tell how deep the chests and the seat are from the elevation. To see why, let's take a closer look at how they are drawn. Elevations are detailed drawings of walls. They show every part of the wall as it would appear straight on. The "eye-people" in Figure 10-2, who consist only of a huge eye and antennae supported by two unbending legs with big feet, show how they see and how an elevation should be drawn. The eye-people see only what is directly in front of them: there is no way that they can see any other part of the object before them, unless they jump to another step. An elevation, like the drawing in Figure 10-1, shows a composite view of how the eye-people would see a wall, from floor to ceiling.

The "Eye-people"

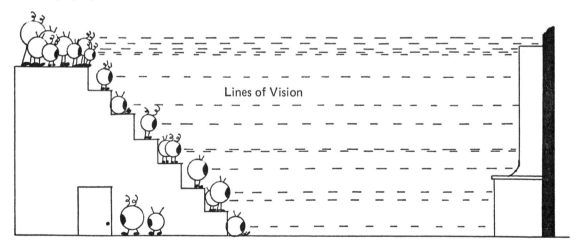

Figure 10-2.

An elevation shows no depth because it is not a perspective drawing. To convince yourself, in case you are a "show-me" type, close one eye and what you see with the other eye will have no depth. It is easy to see objects, but telling how far away they are is not so easy. Elevation drawings likewise do not show an entirely realistic view of the objects they illustrate. Perspective drawings, later in this book, present a more realistic view.

Before reading further, fill in Worksheets 42 and 43.

HOW TO DRAW ELEVATIONS

To draw an elevation, draw the outline of the wall on the paper. Measure the length and height of the wall. Let's say that you want to draw a wall composed primarily of furnishings for a home office. As you would for a floor plan drawing of an existing space, go to the wall and sketch it. The sketch should be accurate enough to include all details, but it need not be dimensionally perfect. Your sketch of this wall might look like Figure 10-3.

Figure 10-3.

Next, you would measure the length and height of everything on the wall. Remember the human needs and values that influenced their placement. Record your measurements on the sketch just made. It now might look like Figure 10-4.

Before proceeding, take a look at Figure 10-5. With a little less care, this is what Figure 10-4 might look like. It illustrates, once again, the necessity to keep all drawings and sketches neat. A lot of mistakes could result from the mess that is Figure 10-5. *Neatness counts.* Don't make even a rough sketch be unreadable, no matter how insignificant the drawing seems.

In order to draw an elevation, you must know the length and height of the wall. Then you can draw an outline of the wall in scale, illustrating the wall's height and width, as shown in Figure 10-6. It's just a box right now.

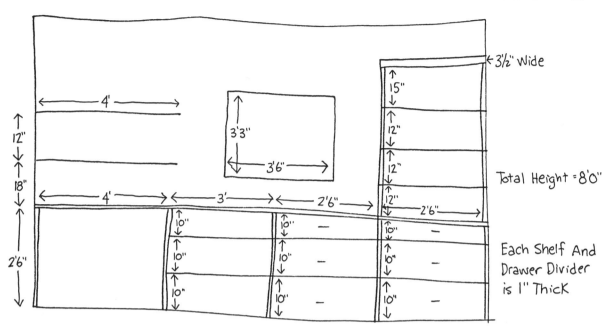

Figure 10-4.

Figure 10-5.

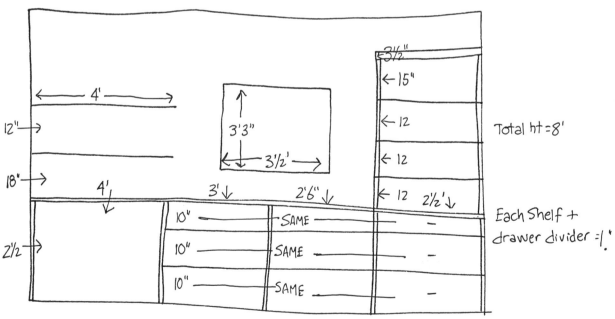

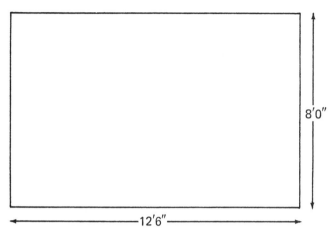

Figure 10-6.

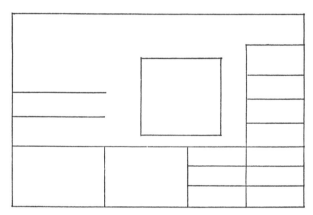

Figure 10-7.

Figure 10-8.

Now begin to add the details. Using the architectural drafting equipment, outline the major aspects of the wall, as shown in Figure 10-7. Then fill in the detail, maybe with books, hardware, wood grain, plants, and so on, to make it realistic (see Figure 10-8). The elevation can be a valuable design illustration when it is colored in and detailed as much as possible. It can present a very convincing picture of the design solution.

Notice a very important aspect of Figure 10-8. Can you tell by looking at the elevation that the desk has a slant top? From an elevation, it is impossible to know what kind of top it has because you do not see perspective. All you can tell is that there is *something else* to this desk. The total height of the slant top is apparent, and that gives a clue as to its detail, but otherwise, there is no hint. Remember that this is a characteristic of elevations.

Well, that is really all there is to drawing an elevation. We have seen only interior elevations here, but you can also do exterior views. Like the type shown here, the purpose of the exterior view is to show wall detail. Figure 10-9 is an example.

When drawing an elevation, include not only the objects that rest directly against the wall but also anything that is within a few feet of the wall: anything that we would normally consider to be a part of the wall's furnishings, particularly furniture that rests against it.

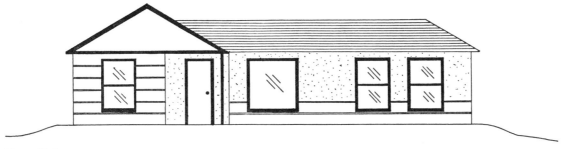

Figure 10-9.

DRAWING SOMETHING THAT HAS BEEN PLACED IRREGULARLY IN A SPACE

Because of special tastes and needs, people do not always place objects squarely within a space. Take, for instance, a favorite large chair that sits diagonally in a corner for convenient television watching. How do you draw this chair on an elevation since you do not see it "straight on"?

Figures 10-10 through 10-16 show how to do this. First, you need a floor plan that includes an outline of the object in its appointed place, such as the one represented in Figure 10-10. Next, measure the distances from each corner of the object to the nearest wall. Number each line for easy future reference, as shown in Figure 10-11.

Now, to draw the object in the elevation, *lightly* sketch four vertical lines that correspond to the measurements you just ascertained. These four lines represent the distances from each corner of the object to the wall. See Figure 10-12. Label these lines with the same numbers used in Figure 10-11.

Determine the height details of the object. If the object is a chair, record its overall height as well as its seat height. Draw these heights horizontally in the elevation, crossing all four vertical lines in doing so, as Figure 10-13 shows.

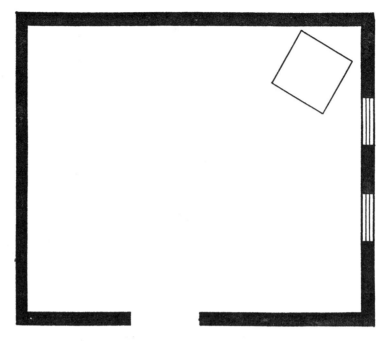

Scale: 1/4″ = 1′0″

Figure 10-10.

Figure 10-11.

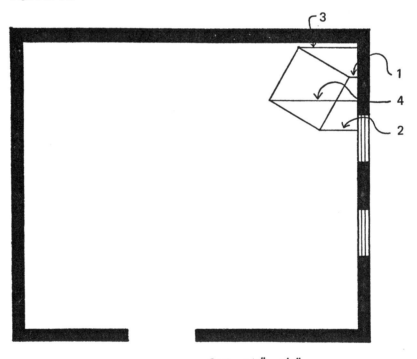

Scale: 1/4″ = 1′0″

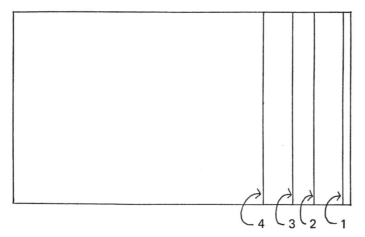

Figure 10-12.

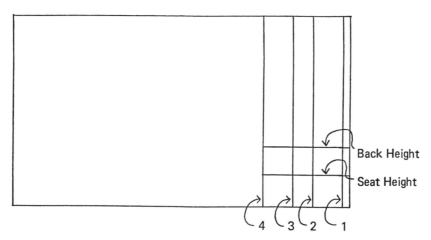

Figure 10-13.

Figure 10-14.

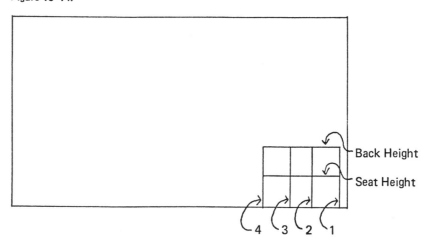

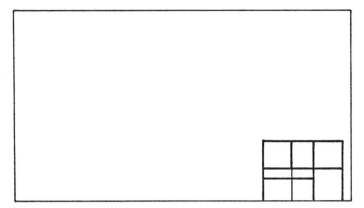

Figure 10-15.

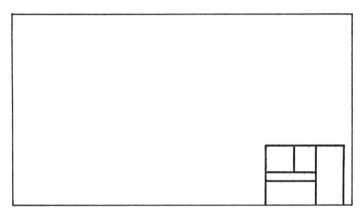

Figure 10-16.

Erase the extra lines above the chair's ultimate height line, as these might cause confusion later. Use the lines you have now as the guidelines. Figure 10-14 illustrates this step. Next, fill in detail, as shown in Figure 10-15, and erase all guidelines. You should have a "realistic" chair, like the one you see in Figure 10-16. This is about as realistic as this chair is going to look in an elevation, considering the fact that neither the seat nor other depth features will be visible.

You can use the same technique for any object. The variation would occur with Figure 10-14, where you add detail. You would draw the detail the same way, but the characteristics naturally would be different.

THE IMPACT OF HUMAN BEHAVIOR UPON ELEVATIONS

Be prepared to draw objects that are placed irregularly in a space because people tend to arrange furniture this way. Elevations, of course, are directly related to human behavior, since they illustrate spaces that human preferences have created. For example, for a conversation area, which configuration in Figure 10-17 might be more appropriate, *a* or *b*? In a conversation, eye contact is very important. People like to look at each other when

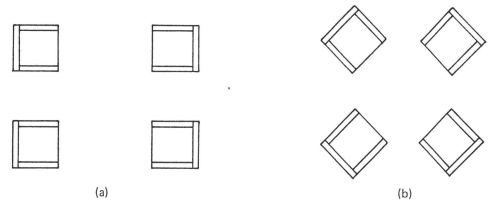

(a)   (b)

Figure 10-17.

they talk. Therefore, *b* may be a better arrangement because it would allow each person to make eye contact with the others. (Chapter 4 discussed this need at greater length.) In an elevation drawing, you may have to draw two of the seats illustrated in Figure 10-17. You would draw each of them as shown in Figures 10-10 through 10-16.

When you are drawing a wall that is not continuous (one that includes a section that is set back from the main part of the wall), you must include in the elevation all sections of the wall. The floor plan in Figure 10-18 shows all the wall sections that will be drawn, and Figure 10-19 shows an elevation drawing of the walls that are dimensioned. Notice that it shows the entire length of the wall. Only a vertical line from floor to ceiling shows where one part of the wall ends and the other begins. This is a drawback to elevations, since it gives no idea which section of the wall is forward of the other. Perspective drawing, the subject of Chapters 12–14, illustrates how to show the relative location of such walls

Figure 10-18.

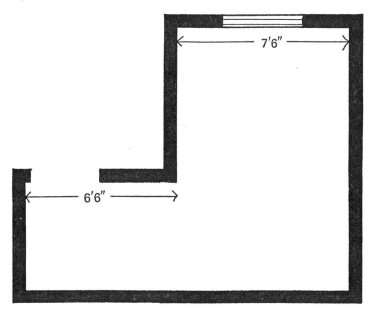

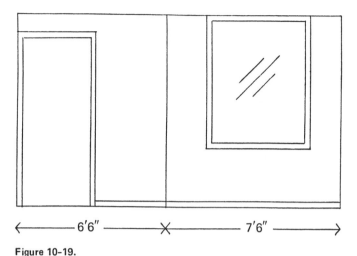

Figure 10-19.

more realistically. For the time being, just concentrate on *detail*, which is the purpose of elevations.

The task description and task analysis that follow reiterate the steps involved in elevation drawing. Use them when completing Worksheets 44 and 45 and future elevation drawings.

TASK DESCRIPTION AND TASK ANALYSIS

Task Description

Given all of the necessary architectural drawing equipment, you will be able to represent a given wall of a space in an elevation drawing in scale on tracing vellum.

Task Analysis

15 steps

1. Collect a tape measure, pencil, and paper, and go to the wall to be drawn.
2. Sketch a preliminary drawing of the wall.
3. Measure and record on the preliminary sketch, in pencil, all wall measurements so that the actual wall measurements correspond to the appropriate lines on the sketch.
4. Verify all measurements by adding together the dimensions of the south end and the north end and comparing them to see that they are equal. Do the same with the east and west ends.
5. Continue to verify the measurements by remeasuring the wall details. Compare them to the original dimensions.
6. If all the measurements check out, go on to the next step. If they do not, then go back to step 3.
7. Assemble all necessary equipment (triangle, T square—if necessary—architect's

scale, small-size tracing vellum, masking tape, pencils, and eraser) on drafting surface.

8. Tape the tracing vellum to the drafting surface with masking tape by placing a small piece of tape over each corner.

9. If you have correctly attached the tracing vellum to the drafting surface, that is, if the bottom edge of the paper is parallel to the bottom edge of the drafting surface, then go on to the next step. If it is not, then go back to step 8, replace the vellum, and retape it.

10. Draw the outer dimensions of the wall, its length and height.

11. Draw the outer dimensions of the largest objects on the wall in the appropriate places, according to their actual placement in the space.

12. Draw the outer dimensions of the smaller objects on the wall according to their actual placement in the space.

13. Draw all details on the wall objects to make the drawing as pictorial as possible.

14. Supply all information requested in the title block.

15. Hand the completed drawing to the instructor on the date assigned.

CHAPTER ELEVEN

MODEL BUILDING

Floor plans and elevations both play important parts in the presentation of a design-solution presentation, but, as with most topics, they are only a beginning. Relying upon these two techniques alone will produce disappointment. Of course, indisputably the most foolproof way to illustrate a design is to build it for the client. Build it on its intended site, in fact: don't just make it as real as possible, make it real! Then invite all the people concerned to the showing, ask for opinions, and change accordingly. If it's all wrong, change it! Just write off the loss on your income taxes, or charge the client for the extra expense!

Does this method sound reasonable? No, it doesn't. And it couldn't be further from what *is* reasonable. Yes, the best way to illustrate a design solution would be to actually construct it, but since it is not feasible, the second best way is to build a scale model of it. In other words, build a dollhouse-size imitation of the house instead of the actual building at the corner of Oak and Cherry Streets.

Model building is a lot of fun. It can be tedious, but it is very absorbing and, if done well, can be a very rewarding way of spending your time. Remember, anyone in a design field is trained to think visually. They should be able to visualize spaces mentally in a way that fairly accurately resembles the area in question. But, again, clients cannot be expected to do the same. If they can, that's fine, but do not count on it. To stimulate the visual sense of laypersons, models come in handy. People can look at it and see everything as it would exist in life, only in miniature. Floor plans and elevations show limited, though important views, and they are both essential in the creation of a model. Models present as realistic and accurate a picture of a design solution as can be expected, short of the actual project itself.

There are not many rules to follow when building models. Often you are on your own, and almost anything goes. *Anything!* In model building, as in love and war, there are no holds barred. Let's take a look at how to build a model.

Begin, or rather *resume*, the design process in the floor plan stage. After completing all the preliminary cerebral work and formulating the schematic drawing, architecturally

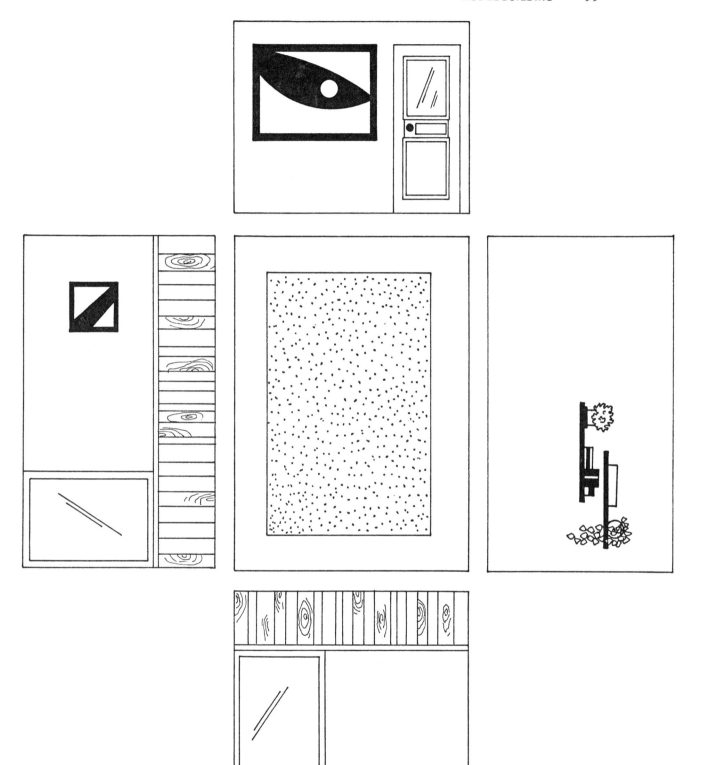

Figure 11-1.

draft the floor plan in scale. Warning: when building a model, avoid using a scale larger than one-half inch. Larger models tend to look, well, bad. The amount of detail needed to make it realistic is just too great, and the result is usually a disaster. Not always, of course, but often enough to make you think. Half-inch and three-eighths inch scales work fine, but anything smaller than quarter-inch scale is quite difficult to handle. The smaller the scale, the more leeway there is for detail. It can be "faked" more. For instance, for a model built in quarter-inch scale, wood trim may be simulated with plain brown paint, but in half-inch scale it may be necessary to use actual wood since it will be more visible and should be more authentic.

Start with the floor plan that specifies only wall, door, and window placement. All of these drawings can be on regular paper or on a heavier board that you can cut out later. Paper would be adhered to a board later for strength, which is a requirement in model building. Next, draw elevations of each wall to show only architectural features again. Omit

Figure 11–2.

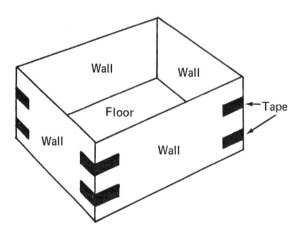

furnishings and other decorative items for now because you will cover the floor plan and elevations with appropriate finishing materials later.

To begin with, you are going to construct a shell: a small replica of the space as it would look unpainted, unfurnished, and completely unfinished. On a piece of board, perhaps *illustration* board, on which you drew the floor plan and elevations or on which you will mount them, you should now see detail similar to Figure 11-1, depending, of course, upon the space itself. In the middle of Figure 11-1 is a floor plan. The accompanying walls surround it. Each section is as complete as it should be at this point. (Note: you can show windows two ways. The one used in Figure 11-1 is to draw the window and illustrate the view that the window would provide. The other method is to cut out the panes of glass and use acetate as the "glass" in the model. This technique is more realistic, but requires a very steady hand to cut the board straight. Both methods are acceptable.)

The next step is to put the pieces together to get an idea of how everything fits. Figure 11-2 shows how to do this. Use masking tape for this trial run.

Once you are sure that all the pieces fit together, dismantle it. Now the fun begins! Start looking for finishing materials for the space: carpeting, wallpaper, wood paneling, whatever you need. It could take some doing to find everything because you must use small-scale patterns. Remember the scale you are working in and choose patterns accordingly. The smaller the better. If you are looking for a particular type of wallpaper pattern, for instance, in half- or quarter-inch scale, a small tweed might illustrate it quite well. You do not have to find materials for everything. You can simply paint walls, if you want them painted, or draw on wallpaper. Acrylic paint is best for painted walls because it dries hard and fast and it will usually not warp the board. Use it full strength rather than watering it down.

After you have selected all your materials, apply them to the unfinished floor plan and elevations. If the space is to be painted, assemble the "room" before painting it so that you can fill in the cracks in the corners of the model with paint. Mount wallpaper on the walls before you assemble them for best results. After you have applied everything, added the architectural features, and cut out the doors and windows, if you have decided to do that,

Figure 11-3.

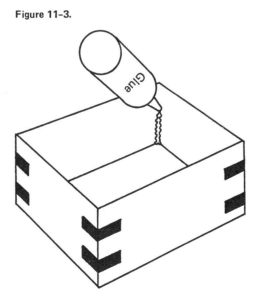

reassemble the pieces by taping them together, as before. Then place the model on a piece of scrap paper and join all of the seams with a clear-drying glue (Figure 11-3). This method will strengthen the model measurably. Once the glue has dried, remove the tape.

What now exists is a space with everything except furnishings, which give you the opportunity to have more fun! Imagination and creativity, as well as patience and tenacity, are really stretched to the limit at this stage. More than any other illustrative technique, model building requires true, *unabashed devotion*. The desire to finish must exceed the frustration that you will undoubtedly encounter during construction.

Generally speaking, the simpler the style of furniture, the easier it will be to build. Straight lines are naturally easier to cut out than are curved ones. Potential furnishing materials include illustration board, balsa wood, and whatever odds and ends seem appropriate. Balsa wood is excellent for making antique furniture because it is easy to carve. You can also use thin sheets of it for flooring and wall paneling. Some patterns for furnishings, along with illustrations of the finished pieces, are in Worksheet 45 of this book for reference. Again, anything is acceptable. Don't be above saving wooden thread spools to use as tables, toothpaste caps for lampshades, large wooden beads for lamp bases, tiny plastic plant leaves and flowers for model greenery, and so forth. Toothpicks can double as bamboo: use them for making window shades. Aluminum foil makes good mirrors. These are just some suggestions: see what is possible. *Try everything. Exploit your imagination!* The task description and task analysis in this section provide a step-by-step description of model building for future reference.

Admittedly, there is not a great deal of direction here for model building, for two main reasons. One is that there are so many ideas that you can use in model building that each project requires individual imagination to develop it. If all the "rules" for model building were listed here, you might repress some innovative thoughts in favor of an "accepted" way of doing something. Besides—and this is reason number two—whether or not anyone could compile a complete list of rules is very difficult to say: does one exist? Consequently, as a model builder, you are pretty much on your own. Remember how to be creative and you should not have too much trouble.

TASK DESCRIPTION AND TASK ANALYSIS

Task Description

Given all of the necessary equipment, you will be able to represent a given space as a model in scale, according to instructions given in class.

Task Analysis

14 steps
1. Collect all materials necessary for drawing a floor plan and an elevation, according to the task analyses that appeared in the two previous chapters. You will also need rubber cement and scissors. Substitute illustration board for paper.
2. Select or create a space for which you want to build a model—confine yourself to one single space for this exercise.

3. Draw an accurate floor plan of the space in scale.
4. Draw accurate elevations of all of the walls in the space in the same scale as the floor plan. Include only architectural details.
5. Cut out the floor plan and elevations.
6. Assemble the floor plan and elevations for proper fit. Remedy any problems *now*.
7. Select materials for all of the decorative aspects of the space (floor, walls, windows, and so on).
8. Cut out all the materials that you have selected in the proper size and shape for the model.
9. Apply all chosen materials to the appropriate surfaces with paper cement.
10. Put the elevations and floor plan together as illustrated earlier in this chapter. Tape it first, and then glue all the seams.
11. Using illustration board, build whatever furnishings exist in or are appropriate for the space. Refer to Worksheet 45 to this section for suggestions.
12. Add detail to the furnishings to make them as real as possible. Use any suitable materials that you can find. Be ruthlessly imaginative!
13. Arrange the furnishings in the space as you would like them to be.
14. If you do not want the furnishings to move, adhere them to the floor of the space.

CHAPTER TWELVE

PERSPECTIVE DRAWING: THE VANISHING POINT

Until now, the visuals that we have been dealing with have been two-dimensional; that is, they illustrate spaces in a flat way. Think about the floor plan. It shows only the length and width of everything. We cannot get a sense of the height of objects from it, so height is the missing third dimension. And what about the elevation? This drawing illustrates height and *either* length or width. Again, only two dimensions. And an elevation shows no depth. A model, of course, shows depth, but it is not a drawing.

Perspective drawing shows three dimensions. It is the most popular method of illustrating a three-dimensional space on a two-dimensional plane, which is represented by the drawing paper. We will explore two types of perspective drawing in this book: one-point and two-point perspectives. First, however, we must talk about the vanishing point, or as it may also be called, the perspective point. The *vanishing point*, or *VP*, as we will call it from now on, gives a perspective drawing its individuality. Its placement determines the view of the space that you plan to show. Consider a box, since it is very easy to imagine a box and then we can transfer the same principle to other, more complicated structures. The placement of the VP will determine what, if any, sides of the box will be visible. The VP does not have to rule you, though. Actually, you control it and use it to the best advantage. You can place the VP wherever it will enhance the drawing most.

Let's take just a minute before going on to think about how we see and what we mean by "perspective." Looking only with one eye distorts vision somewhat. An untrained person has considerable difficulty telling depth perception, or how far away objects are and how fast they are moving, with one eye. On the other hand, the simultaneous use of two eyes allows people to place objects in space since their fields of both eyes cross, as Figure 12-1 illustrates. One-eyed viewing presents a limited view of an object, a flat view. Two-eyed viewing provides us with two simultaneous looks at an object and allows us to determine its spatial position.

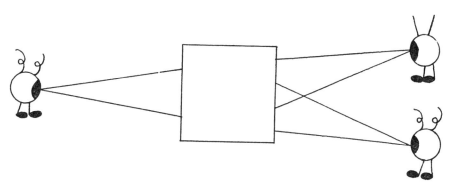

One-eyed Seeing—
Allows One View of
the Object, Is "Flat"

Two-eyed Seeing—
Allows Two Views of the
Object, Is "Dimensional"

Figure 12-1.

Now, about the VP. Its placement *will* determine the view of the object that you will see. It is very easy to remember where to put the VP. Five principles explain how to do it:

1. To show only the front of an object, put the VP behind the object.
2. To show the top of an object, put the VP above it.
3. To show the bottom of an object, put the VP below it.
4. To show the left side of an object, put the VP to the left of it.
5. To show the right side of an object, put the VP to the right of it.

Worksheet 46 provides experience in VP placement. There are nine "boxes" illustrated on that page, and the directions are to draw *all* of them the same size in perspective, utilizing the VP in the center of the box in the middle as the guide. A sample of that exercise and how to do it appear here.

Figure 12-2 shows the middle box, complete with the VP, surrounded by two boxes to be drawn in perspective. The first step in putting the two boxes into perspective is to

Figure 12-2.

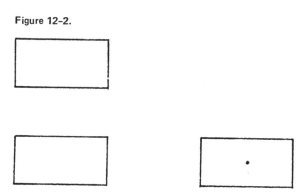

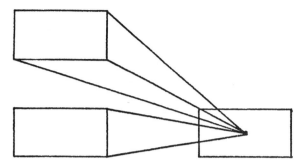

Figure 12-3.

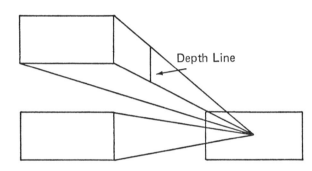

Figure 12-4.

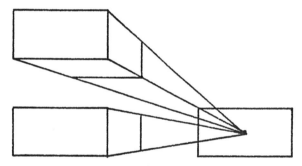

Figure 12-5.

draw lines from the VP to corners of the boxes, as shown in Figure 12-3. Note that you do not draw lines to *every* corner since, if these boxes are opaque, some lines will be hidden. They are the ones that do not appear at this time.

Figure 12-4 shows how to indicate depth in the box. For the purpose of this exercise, the depth is arbitrary. Since all of the boxes are the same size, this first *depth line* is the guide for all of the other lines that we will add. Figure 12-5 illustrates all of the necessary depth lines. Notice that the sides of the boxes, represented by the vertical lines, are all *perfectly vertical*, while the bottoms of the boxes, represented by horizontal lines, are *perfectly horizontal*. When completing this exercise, use drafting equipment so that you can make all of the boxes the same size.

The next step is to erase that part of each line that you no longer need. What remains

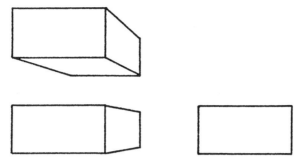

Figure 12-6.

is illustrated in Figure 12-6. How many boxes appear in perspective? Two? Three? Actually, there are three. If you want to show only the front of an object, put the VP directly behind it. The box with the VP "inside" it, then, *is* drawn in perspective.

Vanishing points are important in both one-point and two-point perspective drawing. One-point perspective utilizes one VP while two-point perspective has two. The reasons will surface in the next two chapters. But the five principles of vanishing point placement apply to all perspective drawing, so remember them.

CHAPTER THIRTEEN

ONE-POINT PERSPECTIVE DRAWING

Floor plans and elevations are indispensable to a design presentation. Builders also need them in order to know what to construct. But what will sell a design? What about people who do not know what these drawings mean: what will get their attention? Less architectural drawings that show what the space will look like when it is completed will usually do the trick. These drawings are called "perspectives."

We will treat one-point perspectives first. They are called "one-point perspectives" because almost all of the diagonal lines that exist in the sketch emanate from *one* vanishing point, or perspective point (see Chapter 12). One-point perspectives illustrate three walls of a space. They are particularly useful in illustrating a very long, narrow area or to show off one wall of a space that is considerably more interesting than the rest. In any case, choose the most interesting wall as the *focal* wall of the drawing. It will contain the VP. The VP will be on the drawing's *horizon line*, which is the level on the drawing at which all lines seem to disappear. An example is a highway or railroad that travels ahead over a hill or a relatively flat plain. The sides of the highway or rails of the railroad will "meet" on the horizon line. Or at least will seem to meet. Figure 13-1 illustrates where the horizon line and the VP would occur.

There are many methods for drawing perspectives. The "two" presented in this book really are the same: two-point perspective drawing really relies upon the same technique as one-point does. The method is a very simple one for a specific reason. It is a method designed to bring an awareness of three-dimensional illustration principles to the person who will draft the space. The ultimate goal is to be able to adequately free-hand sketch a space at a later time. Architectural drafting this is not! You will use architectural tools in the process and the result may appear to be architectural, depending upon the individual's interpretation, but the method actually is far from architectural. In short, this method is meant to be quick and simple, yet accurate. The illustrator depends only upon himself. Another advantage over the more analytical type of drawing is that minimal architectural drafting equipment is necessary.

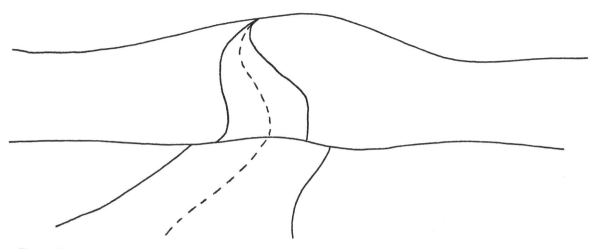

Figure 13-1.

DRAWING ONE-POINT PERSPECTIVES

You begin one-point perspectives, in effect, by drawing an elevation of the most interesting wall in the space that is being designed. So measure the length and height of the wall that you have chosen to be the focal wall of the illustration. Then determine what scale to use and draw the wall to scale, as in Figure 13-2.

Next, draw the two adjacent walls. Remember the five principles of vanishing point placement because they affect the adjacent walls:

1. To show only the front of an object, put the VP behind the object.
2. To show the top of an object, put the VP above it.
3. To show the bottom of an object, put the VP below it.
4. To show the left side of an object, put the VP to the left of it.
5. To show the right side of an object, put the VP to the right of it.

Figure 13-2.

Scale: 1/4″ = 1′0″

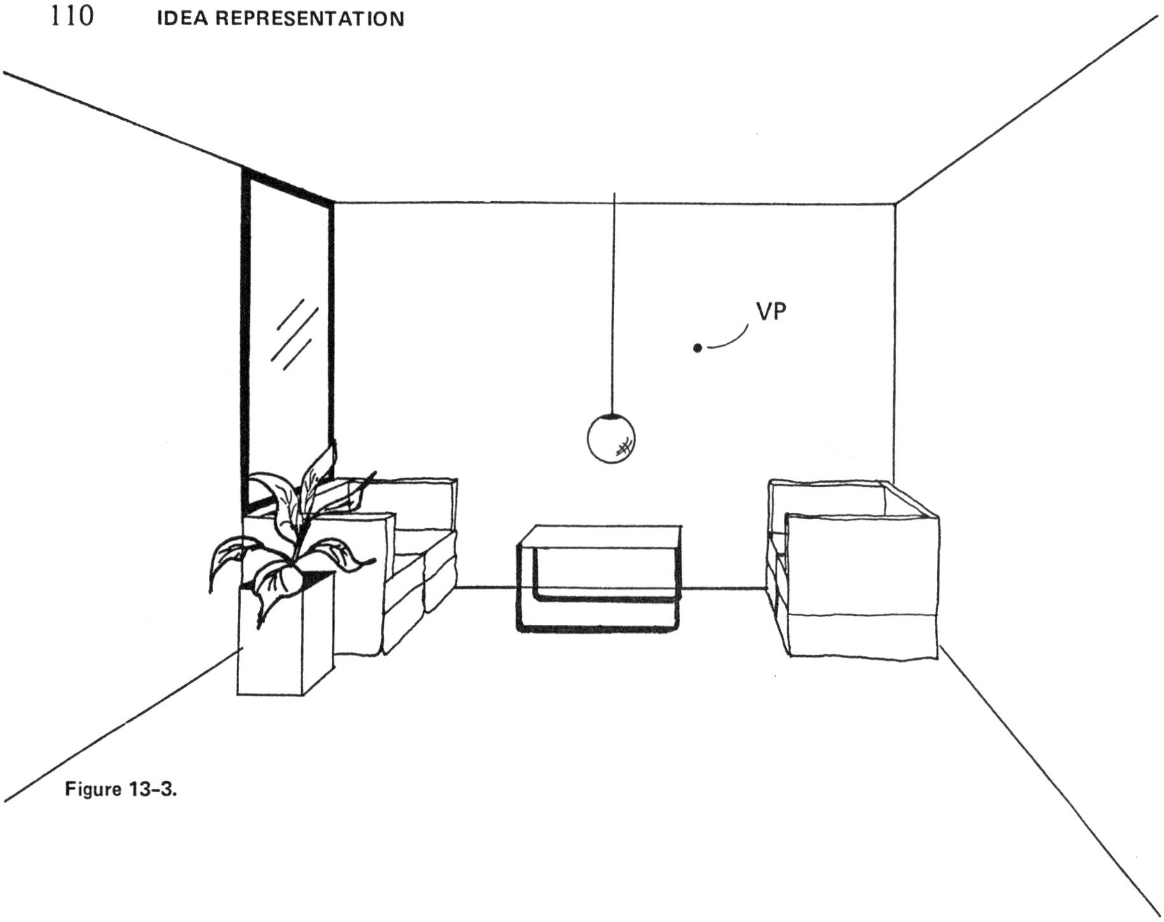

VP

Figure 13-3.

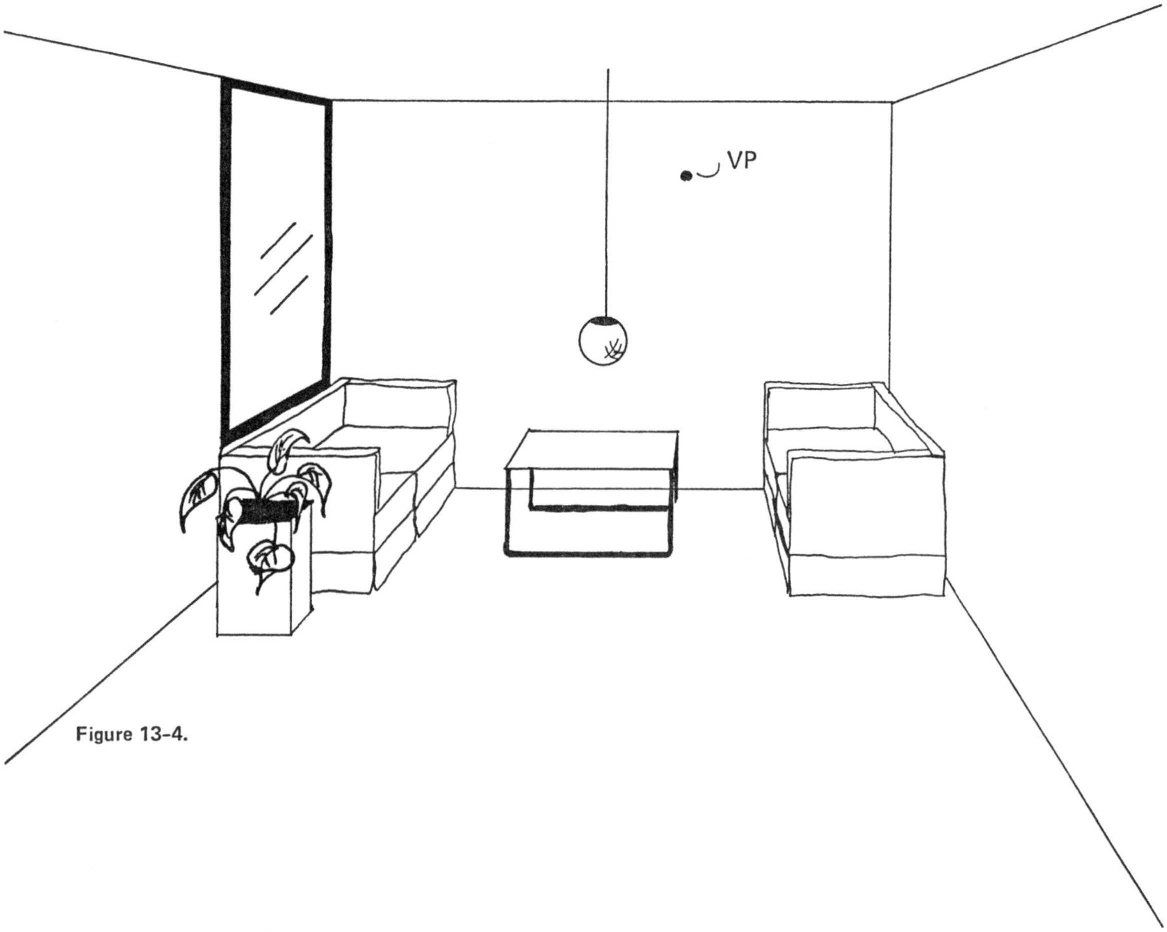

VP

Figure 13-4.

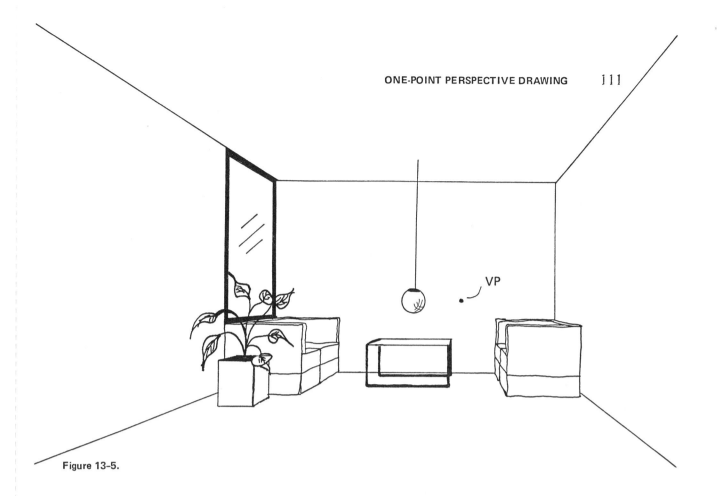

Figure 13-5.

We will implement all of these principles here. Placing the VP on the focal wall is really a matter of deciding what view of the space's interior you want to present. To begin with, select the height of the VP. Now imagine walking into a room and looking at it while you are standing up. An average, eye-level height is five feet or so, so placing the VP this far from the floor would give a normal point of view to the space, as Figure 13-3 shows. This is a normal view, and it is very effective. However, the unusual will often attract more attention and be more effective. The placement of the VP will help you achieve an unusual effect. Placing it close to the ceiling will produce a bird's-eye view, which allows the viewer to see the tops of the objects within the space, as in Figure 13-4. Conversely, placing the VP nearer to the floor, say, within three feet of it, will produce an equally unique effect. The feeling could be likened to the view of a space that someone has while sitting on the floor and looking up. The bottoms of some objects are seen, and the fronts of the objects on the floor are accentuated. Figure 13-5 illustrates this perspective. Similarly, the placement of the VP on the right or left half of the focal wall will also affect the view. Figure 13-6 illustrates the effect of putting the VP left of center.

Note that the wall that is farthest from the VP appears in a more realistic proportion to the focal wall than its opposite wall does. This is a *very important* point because when illustrating a space in one-point perspective, there probably will be one wall adjacent to the focal wall that is quite intriguing, or at least more deserving of immortalization by having its "portrait" drawn than another wall in the space. In that case, place the VP on the side of the focal wall opposite the side you want to show in more detail.

So the next step is to place the vanishing point. Again, its placement depends entirely

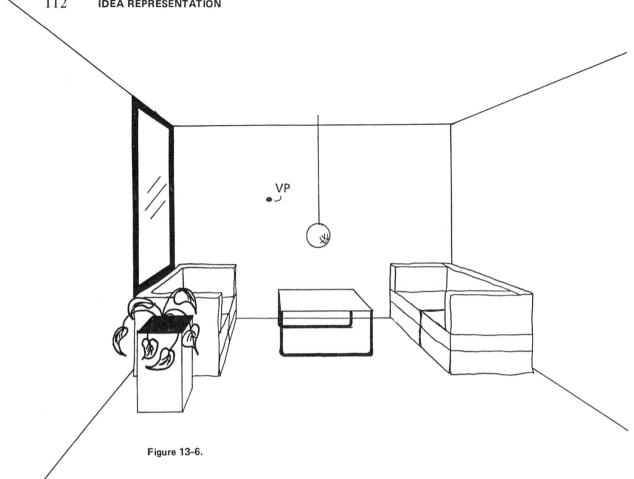

Figure 13–6.

upon the view of the space that you desire to show. There is just one more important point: do not place the VP directly next to a border of the focal wall. Figure 13-7 illustrates a good, relative area in which to confine the VP. Placing it very close to a wall, ceiling, or floor will produce too much distortion within the perspective. Figure 13-8 demonstrates a common result of this practice.

Figure 13–7.

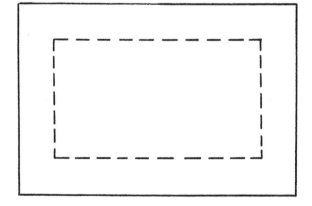

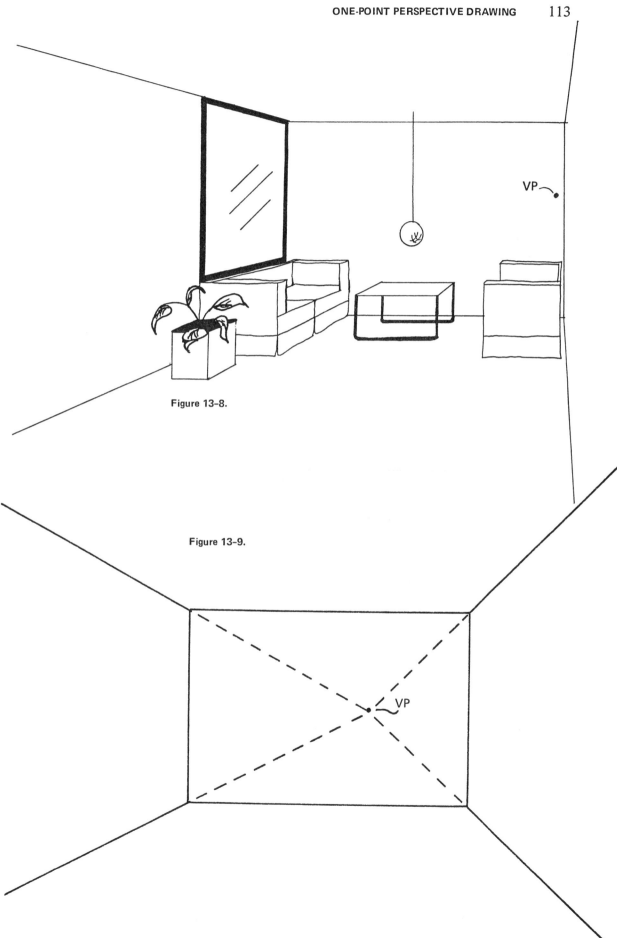

Figure 13-8.

Figure 13-9.

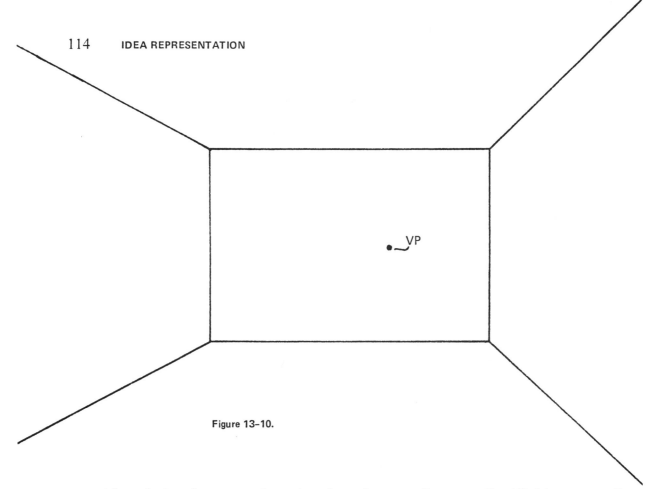

Figure 13-10.

After placing the perspective point, draw the two adjacent walls. All this step entails is using a straight edge to draw straight lines from the VP through and beyond each of the four corners, as Figure 13-9 shows. The sections of the lines drawn within the boundary of the focal wall are broken because they will be erased. Figure 13-10 shows the clean drawing, which looks more like an empty space again.

Right now, do Worksheet 47, which gives practice in drawing the adjacent walls, floor, and ceiling of a space.

FILLING IN THE DETAILS

Next you will add details to the drawing. Again, begin with the focal wall. Draw doors, windows, and all architectural features exactly as you would in an elevation. Draw everything that is flat against or within the focal wall. You need do nothing other than what you would do in an elevation drawing. Figure 13-11 shows an example.

Now repeat the procedure for the two side walls; that is, put in all architectural details that lie on a plane with the wall. Remember that *all measuring in one-point perspective is done on the focal wall*—all of it, without exception. So, to draw objects on the side walls, you measure from the vanishing point through the appropriate heights at the "corners" of the space. Let's say we want a window on the left wall to be four feet high and its base to be two feet off the floor. See Figure 13-12, which shows how to position this window vertically. Now that you have determined where to put the top and bottom of the window you must find its width. This step requires a little guesswork—not much, but it has to be *good-quality* guesswork.

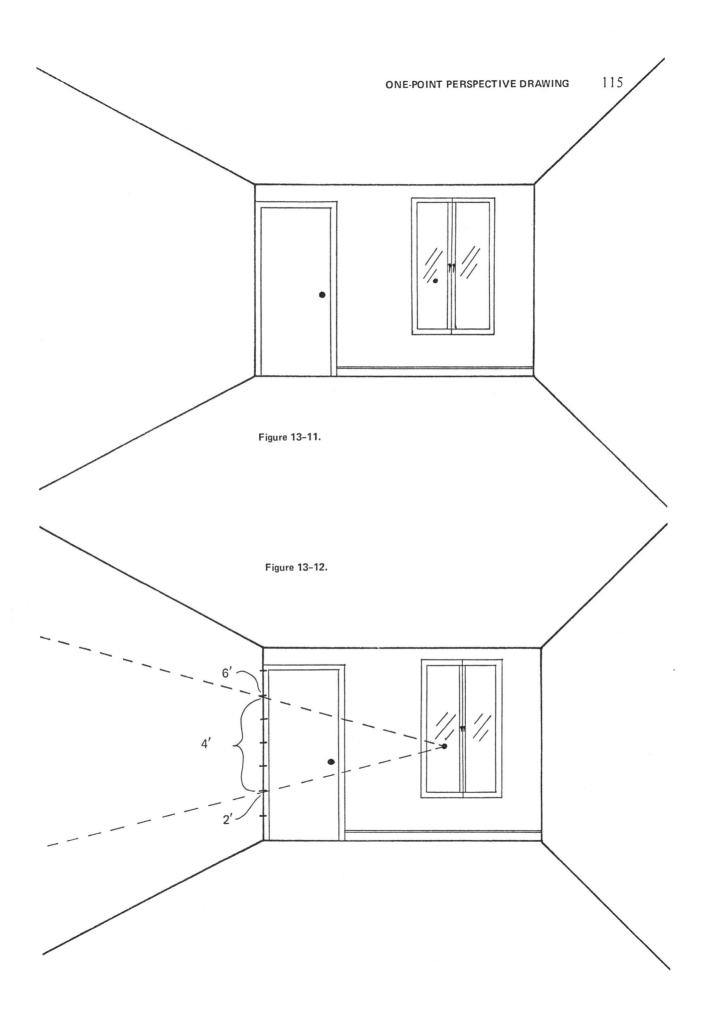

Figure 13–11.

Figure 13–12.

6'

4'

2'

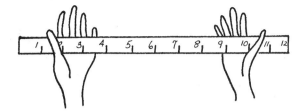

Figure 13–13.

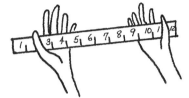

Figure 13–14.

Don't think about the drawing for a minute. Look instead at a ruler, maybe an architect's scale. Hold it directly in front of you so that every inch is visible, as in Figure 13-13. An inch measures an inch, right? Now, turn the ruler sideways a little so that you see it at an angle, as in Figure 13-14. Does an inch still measure an inch? An inch measures an inch no matter how the ruler is held, but actually, the more it is turned, the "shorter" the inches become, especially those farthest away.

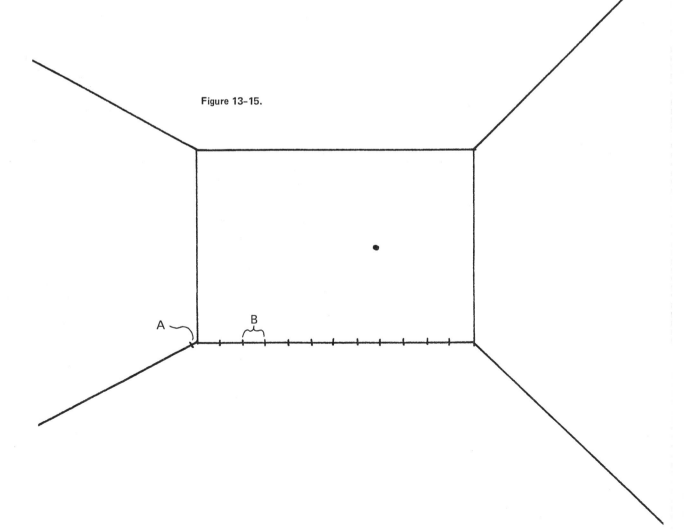

Figure 13–15.

The same happens in perspective drawing. The "farther away" part of the drawing is, the smaller the objects become. On the focal wall, since it faces you squarely, a foot measures a foot. This is a true measurement at all times, so it makes sense to measure everything else by this wall. However, on the side walls, since you are drawing in perspective, you cannot measure the same way as you can on the focal wall. So do it this way: beginning at a corner of the space, measure off a distance equal to one-quarter the distance of a foot on the focal wall, as shown in Figure 13-15.

Distance A equals one-quarter the measurement of a foot on the focal wall (B). Measure about two more spaces just a little larger than the first space, and continue increasing the sizes of the spaces as they go away from the focal wall (see Figure 13-16). Now, remembering Figure 13-12, you can "start and stop" the window. If it begins three feet from the corner of the room and is four feet wide, it will look like Figure 13-17 in perspective. Clean up the drawing so it looks more like Figure 13-18.

To draw something on the right wall, use the markings on the left wall as a guide. Place the T square or parallel bar on the drafting surface at the point of your first "foot" measurement along the left wall. Then make a corresponding mark on the right wall where the horizontal instrument meets the right wall line, as in Figure 13-19. Continue in this fashion to mark the entire length of the wall, as in Figure 13-20. Notice how the markings on the wall closer to the VP are closer together than on the other wall. This is right. Do you know why? Think about it.

The next part of the drawing involves the placement of objects within the space. The next several pages illustrate in step-by-step detail how to do this. When drawing objects,

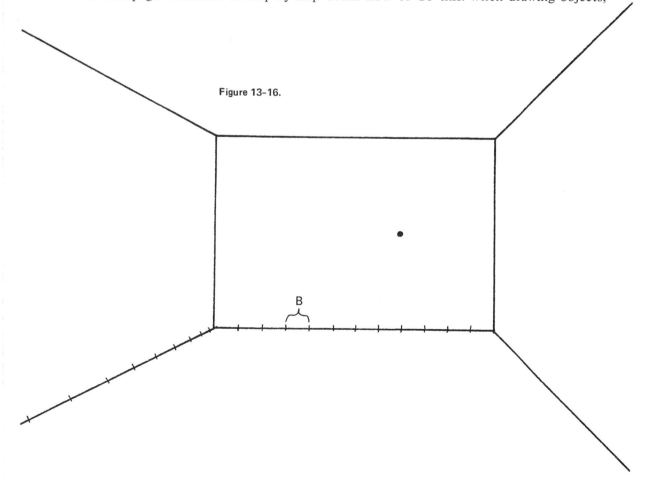

Figure 13-16.

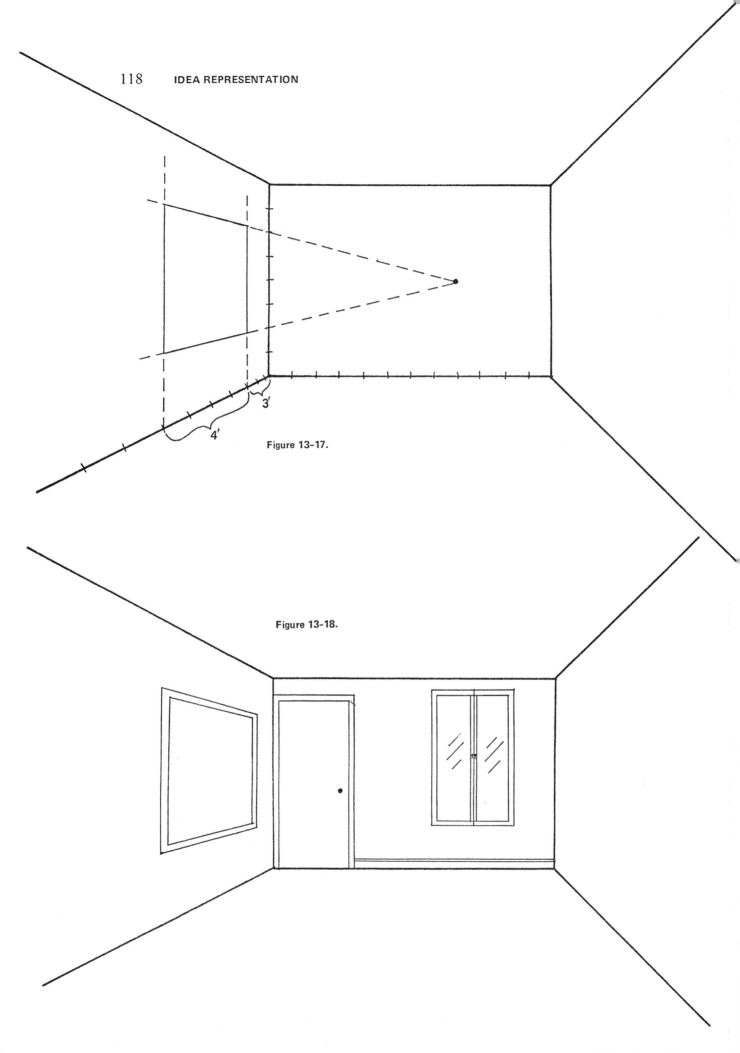

Figure 13–17.

Figure 13–18.

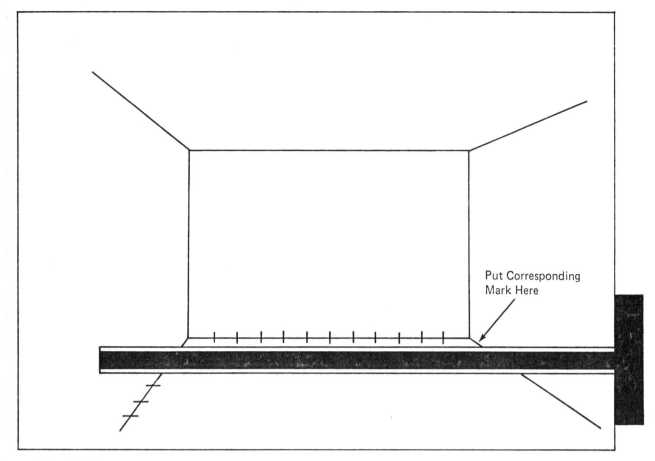

Figure 13–19.

Figure 13–20.

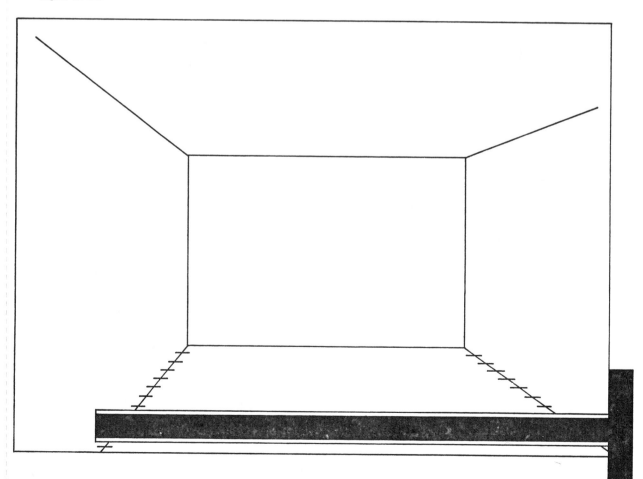

draw only boxes to begin with. You can add detail later. Your primary consideration should be getting the objects in proper scale and proportion to the rest of the drawing. You should avoid spending an undue amount of time filling in minute detail only to realize that it is disproportionate to the space itself. Some illustrations in this section show how to turn plain, ordinary boxes into realistic "furniture."

Another thing before you go on: draw the space's objects in a progressive order, similar to the following sequence:

1. Flat architectural objects, such as doors, windows, and pictures, on the focal wall
2. Flat architectural objects on the side walls
3. Flat objects on the floor and ceiling, such as tiles, area rugs, flush lighting, and so forth
4. Objects on the focal wall that extend out into the space but rest against one wall
5. Objects on the two side walls that extend out into the space but rest against one wall
6. Objects in the middle of the floor that are parallel to two walls
7. Objects that are placed diagonally in the space (this item will be detailed in the next chapter)
8. Fill in floor details wherever needed
9. Fill in ceiling details wherever needed

Now take a look at the next few pages to see how to implement this procedure.

HOW TO DRAW IN ONE-POINT PERSPECTIVE OBJECTS THAT APPEAR ON THE FLOOR OF A SPACE

When drawing objects that extend out into the room from the focal wall (with reference to Figure 13-21):

1. Draw the width and height of the object against the focal wall, as you would in an elevation. (a)
2. Measuring out into the space, according to the foot guidelines that you have established, draw the space that the object occupies on the floor. Do this by drawing a straight line from the vanishing point, through both of the places where the object meets the floor. Extend the lines as far into the space as the established guidelines indicate and then connect them with a horizontal line, which indicates the baseline of the object. (b)
3. Draw vertical lines up from each front "corner." (c)
4. Draw the two top side lines from the vanishing point so that they meet the vertical "corner" lines drawn in step 3. Then complete the box by drawing in the horizontal line that will serve as the top front edge. This line should be perfectly horizontal. It connects the two points at which the vertical front corner lines meet those top side lines as they were placed by the vanishing point. (d)
5. Add necessary detail. (e)

When drawing objects that extend out into the room from a side wall (with reference to Figure 13-22):

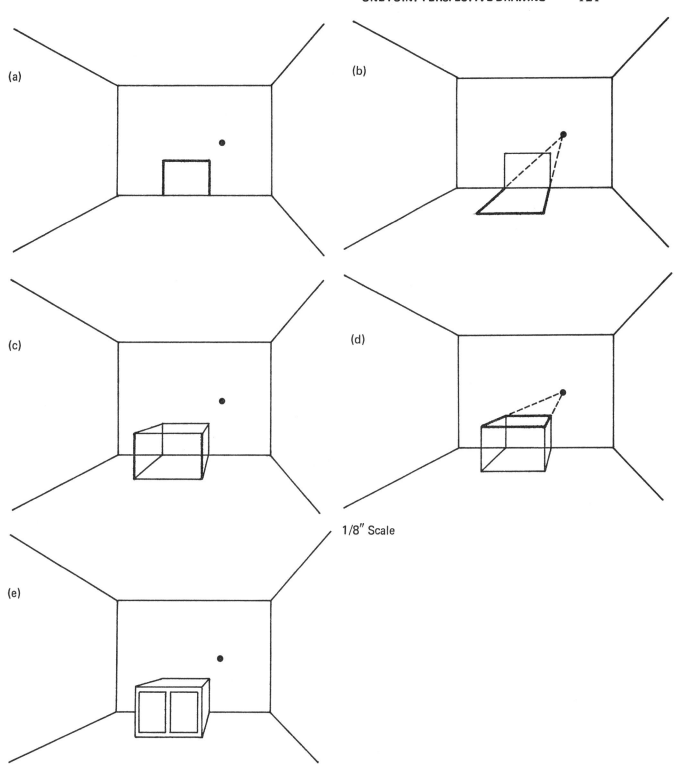

(a)

(b)

(c)

(d)

1/8″ Scale

(e)

Figure 13–21.

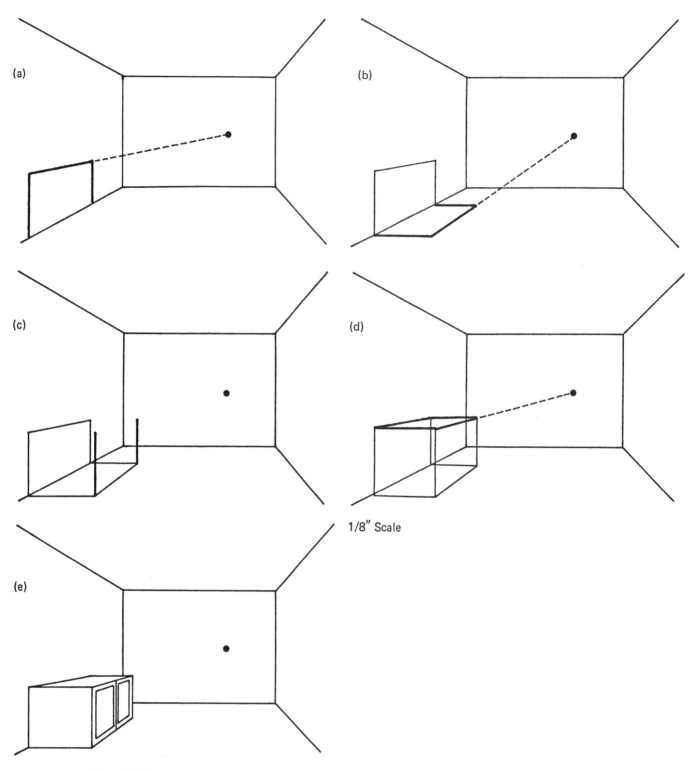

(a)

(b)

(c)

(d)

1/8″ Scale

(e)

Figure 13–22.

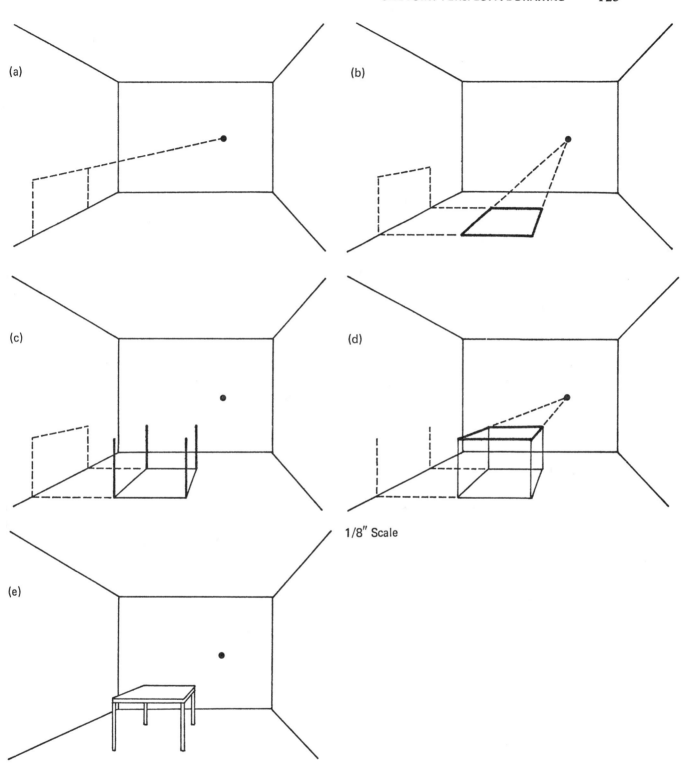

(a)

(b)

(c)

(d)

1/8″ Scale

(e)

Figure 13–23.

1. Begin by measuring the object's distance from the wall and its total length. Make the appropriate vertical lines at these two places. Then draw the object's height with a straight line from the VP through the height of the object as it is measured at the space's corner. For instance, if the object is three feet high, you would draw a line from the VP through the three-foot mark at the room's corner out to where you are drawing the object. (a)

2. Next draw the space the object takes up on the floor. Extend horizontal lines out from each of the two places where the vertical lines you drew in the previous step meet the floor. Then, from the vanishing point through the point on the far wall that marks the width of the object, draw a straight line to connect the two horizontal lines. (b)

3. Draw vertical lines from each "corner." (c)

4. From each top "corner" on the wall draw horizontal lines that are equal in length to their corresponding lines on the floor. Then draw a line from the VP to connect both front "corners" that you just created. (d)

5. Add necessary detail. (e)

When drawing objects that rest in the middle of the floor, away from the focal and side walls, follow the steps just given for drawing objects on a side or focal wall, but *pretend* that the object really is resting against a wall. Draw the size of the object where it will lie in the space along with the distance separating it from the nearest parallel wall. In effect, you will have an elongated object. When you finish, erase the section that represents the space between the object and the wall. This area is shown in Figure 13-23 as broken lines.

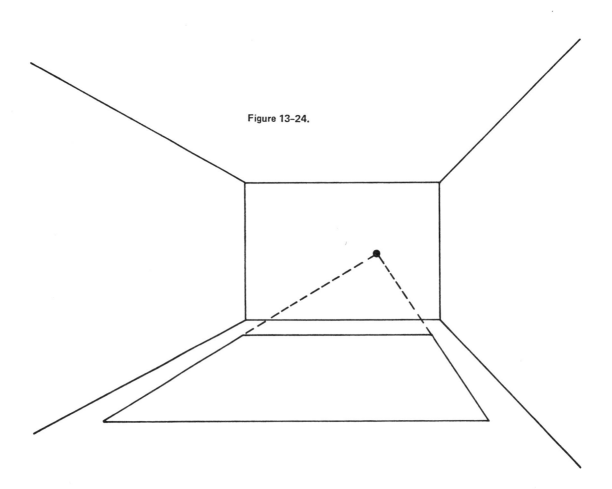

Figure 13-24.

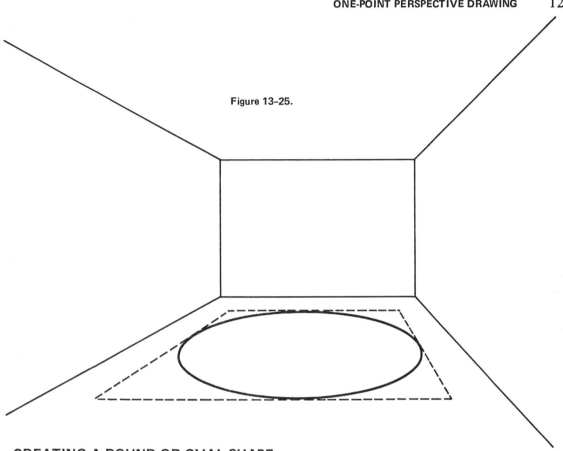

Figure 13-25.

CREATING A ROUND OR OVAL SHAPE
WITHIN A SQUARE OR RECTANGULAR SPACE

Sometimes you may want to show area rugs in a space. Drawing them is really simple. Architecturally draft a square or rectangle using the largest dimensions of the ultimate object to guide you, as Figure 13-24 shows. Then sketch a "circle" or "oval" within the "square" or "rectangle," and you will see the rug in correct perspective to the space, as in Figure 13-25.

TASK DESCRIPTION AND TASK ANALYSIS

Task Description

Given all of the necessary architectural drawing equipment, you will be able to represent a specific space as a one-point perspective in scale.

Task Analysis

16 steps

1. Collect all necessary architectural drafting equipment.
2. Draw a floor plan of an existing or theoretical space or refer to the floor plan in Figure 13-26.

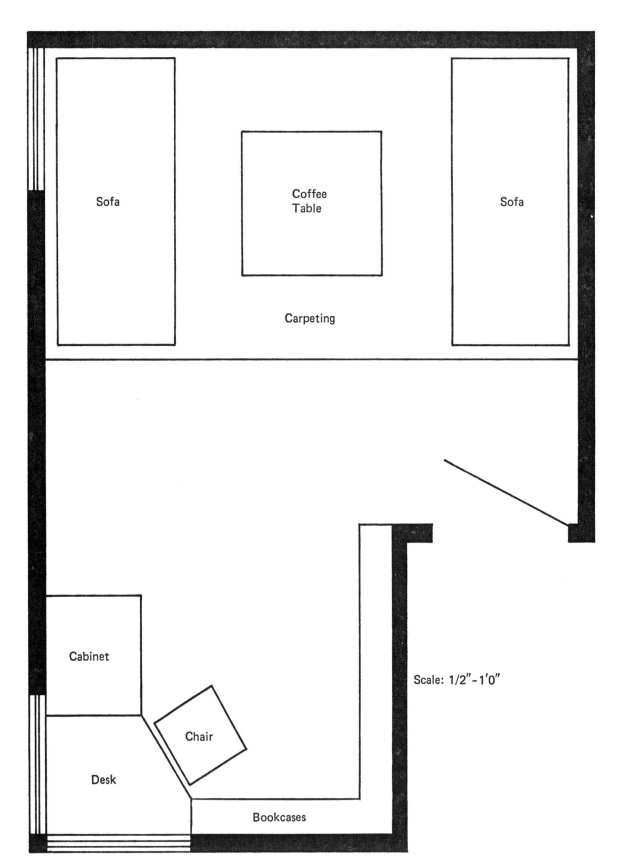

Sofa

Coffee
Table

Sofa

Carpeting

Cabinet

Scale: 1/2″-1′0″

Chair

Desk

Bookcases

Figure 13-26.

3. Select the focal wall.
4. Select a scale to work in.
5. Tape the drawing paper to the drafting surface with masking tape by placing a small piece of tape over each corner.
6. Measure the focal wall and draw it as you would an elevation.
7. Draw the two adjacent walls on your drawing paper, as shown earlier in this chapter.
8. Draw the architectural details, such as doors and windows.
9. Draw in decorative wall details, such as pictures.
10. "Box in" the furnishings on the focal wall.
11. "Box in" furnishings on the side walls.
12. Add detail to the walls and furnishings to make the space appear "lived in."
13. Add shadows and shading to the drawing to make it realistic.
14. Complete the title block in the corner with all the necessary information as described earlier.
15. If you used a space other than the floor plan given in this section, hand in your floor plan and indicate which walls you drew.
16. Hand the completed drawing to the instructor on the date assigned.

CHAPTER FOURTEEN

TWO-POINT PERSPECTIVE DRAWING

Probably the most exciting and dramatic type of illustration discussed in this book is two-point perspective. It is a method of showing how a corner or two walls of a space will look when the design process has been completed. As you will see, you can manipulate the drawing so that you can show selected parts of the space by carefully placing the vanishing points—yes, vanishing *points*. As the name of the drawing implies, a two-point perspective has two perspective points.

The next few pages will take you step-by-step through the process of preparing a two-point perspective. Be cognizant of this fact: one- and two-point perspectives are very similar to draw. Of course, there are some differences, but basically, the principles are the same.

Oh, yes. At the end of this chapter notice also that there is a reference to one-point perspective. It involves drawing an object that is placed "irregularly" in a space, that is, one that is not parallel to any of the walls in a square or rectangular area. This aspect of drawing is discussed here because it actually requires superimposing a two-point perspective drawing on a one-point perspective. Be alert for this special case.

HOW TO DRAW TWO-POINT PERSPECTIVES

Since two-point perspective illustrates two walls, you cannot draw a complete far wall as you can in one-point perspective. The concern of this type of drawing is basically the corner, where two walls meet.

We begin by drawing a vertical line the height of the room in scale. This line, as shown in Figure 14-1, represents the corner of the space being detailed. Before drawing the two walls themselves, you must select the vanishing points. Here is something to remember: the farther away the vanishing points are from the corner line, the more realistic the drawing will be. And, again, in choosing the VPs, you have to decide what point of view you want:

do you want to look up at the space, look down at it, or have a "realistic" eye-level view? Follow the same procedure for placement of the VPs here as in one-point perspective, but keep both VPs on the horizon line.

1/8″ Scale

Figure 14–1.

What is the horizon line? It is a horizontal line that intersects the vertical line at the level you have selected. Other than providing a "home" for the VPs, it is not a part of the drawing. So make this line *very light*. In Figure 14-2, the horizon line, or HL, is three feet above the floor level, but remember that you can put it at *any* level along the corner line.

Horizon line

Figure 14–2.

Then, after locating the HL, place a VP on each side of the corner line. Remember, the farther away from the corner line that you place the VPs, the more realistic the drawing (see Figure 14-3). To draw the two walls, just extend lines from each VP through the top and bottom of the corner line, as indicated in Figure 14-4. After erasing the broken lines and the horizon line (do not erase the VPs until you have finished the drawing) you will have a drawing that looks like Figure 14-5. It looks sort of like a room, doesn't it?

Figure 14–3.

VP   VP

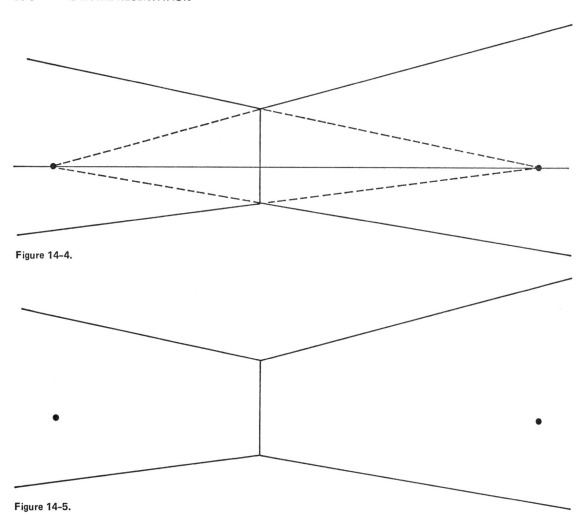

Figure 14-4.

Figure 14-5.

As in one-point perspective, you can manipulate the drawing to show the wall you think is more important. You do this by the placement of the VPs. For instance, if you want to show more of the *left* wall, place the *left VP closer* to the corner line than the right VP. This approach is shown in Figure 14-6. You would do the opposite to show more of the right wall; that is, the right vanishing point would be closer to the corner line than the left one is. Similarly, to show more of the floor than the ceiling, place the vanishing points higher in the drawing. To show more of the ceiling, place them lower.

To make two-point perspectives look more realistic, the first thing to do is to begin adding detail that is flush against the walls, as in one-point perspective. Refer back to Chapter 13 now, if necessary, to see what you did. Proceed similarly here.

Mark off "foot" lines on the corner line in the scale you are using, as you would do on the focal wall in one-point perspective. Then indicate the foot measurements on the baselines of the walls as shown in Figure 14-7. The first "foot" closest to the corner will measure approximately half the size of the "foot" measurement on the corner line itself. Measure about two more spaces the same length as A along the floor line, then gradually increase the length of them as you move away from the corner line. Approximately five

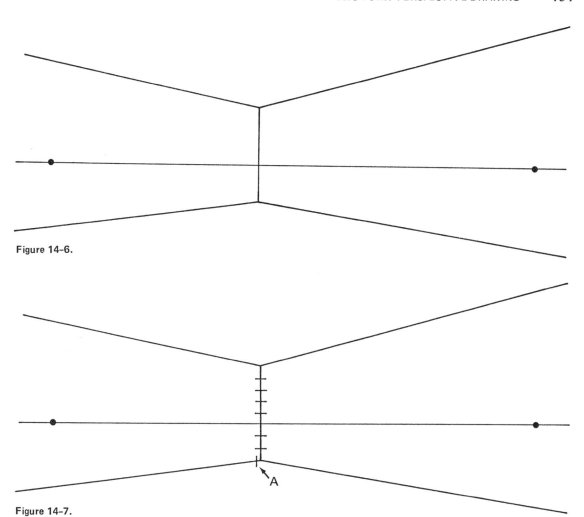

Figure 14–6.

Figure 14–7.

Figure 14–8.

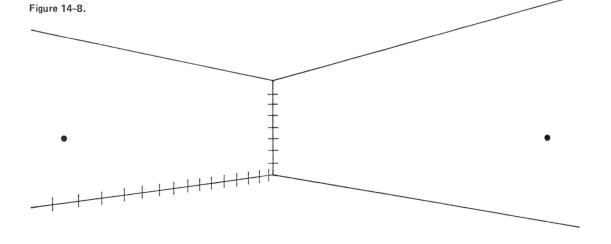

"feet" out from the corner line, the feet should be the same size as they are on the vertical corner line, as shown in Figure 14-8. Actually, the measurement of line A will depend upon the placement of the vanishing points. If both or just one is quite close to the corner line, the first "foot" line on the floor will be equal to about one-fourth the size of the foot measured on the corner line. If the perspective points are farther apart, it will be closer to half the size of the foot measurement. This is another time when you will have to use some good judgment to determine the length of the first line. Figure 14-9 illustrates the flexibility that VP manipulation allows.

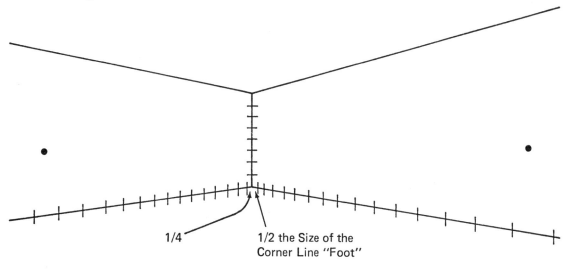

1/4   1/2 the Size of the
Corner Line "Foot"

Figure 14-9.

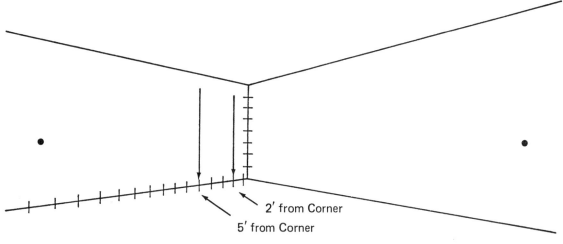

2′ from Corner
5′ from Corner

Figure 14-10.

Now let's say we have a door to draw on the left wall. It is two feet from the corner of the space, three feet wide, and seven feet high. Since this architectural detail occurs on the left wall, the perspective point on the right will be used to draw the top of the door. As in one-point perspective, first draw vertical lines up from the floor as done in Figure 14-10, one at two feet from the corner because the door begins there and one at five feet

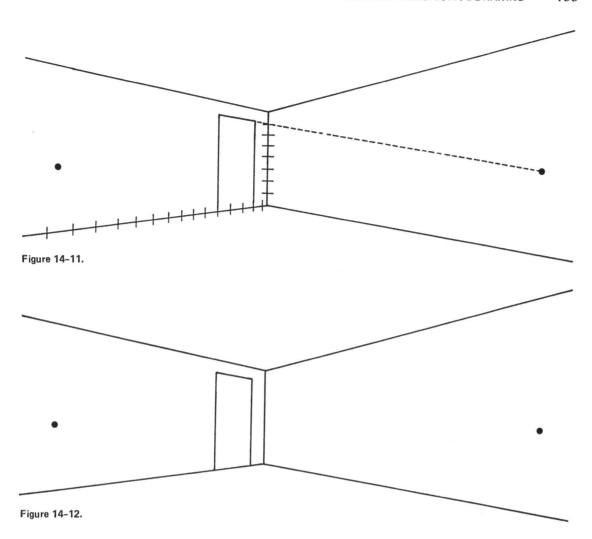

Figure 14–11.

Figure 14–12.

from the corner because the door is three feet wide. Draw a line from the right perspective point through the seven foot mark on the corner line to represent the door's height and connect the two vertically drawn lines (see Figure 14-11). Erase the extra lines, and the result will resemble Figure 14-12.

To draw a similar detail on the right wall, follow the same procedure, but reverse it. Use the perspective point on the left to draw the top and, if necessary, the bottom of the object. For examples, see Figures 14-13–14-15.

Why is the perspective point on the left used to draw details on the right wall and the perspective point on the right to draw details on the left wall? Write your answer here.

_____

_____

_____

_____

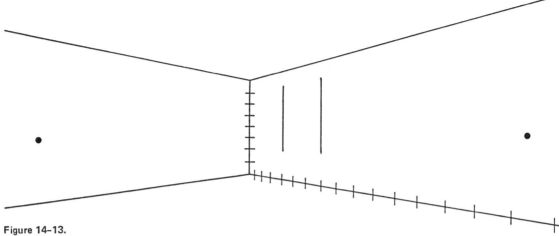

Figure 14–13.

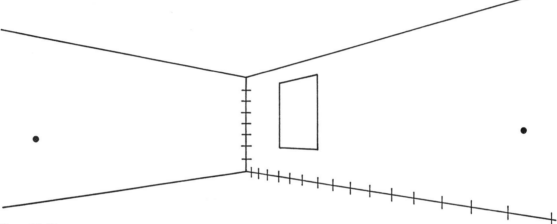

Figure 14–14.

Figure 14–15.

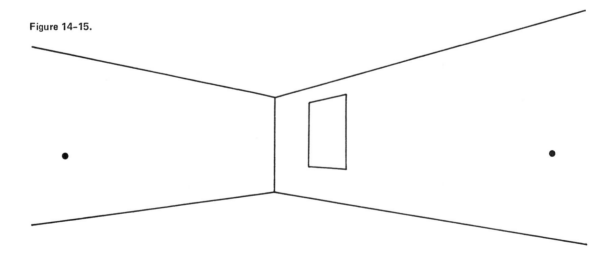

Now, before we see how to draw objects within the space, consider the following: how do you *know* what perspective point you will use? This is the most critical factor in perspective drawing, and understanding it will simplify the process immeasurably. So pay attention and you will see how the technique helps make the drawing process logical. But also remember this: *draw first* and *ask questions later!* This practice helps, too!

Back to the question, "How do you know what perspective point you will use?" Very simple. For every line on the floor plan that is parallel to the right-hand wall, use the left perspective point. Conversely, for every line parallel to the left-hand wall, use the right perspective point. The floor plan in Figure 14-16 details this principle. Drawing the bed shown in Figure 14-16 would give something like Figure 14-17. All lines emanating from the right perspective point are parallel to the left-hand wall in reality, and all lines from the left perspective point are actually parallel to the right-hand wall.

Figure 14-18 shows in step-by-step detail how to draw an object against a wall. Figure

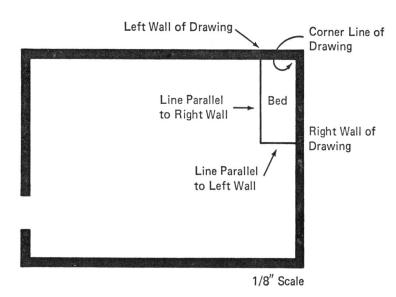

Figure 14-16.

Figure 14-17.

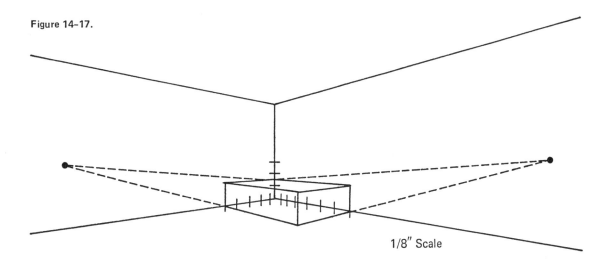

1/8″ Scale

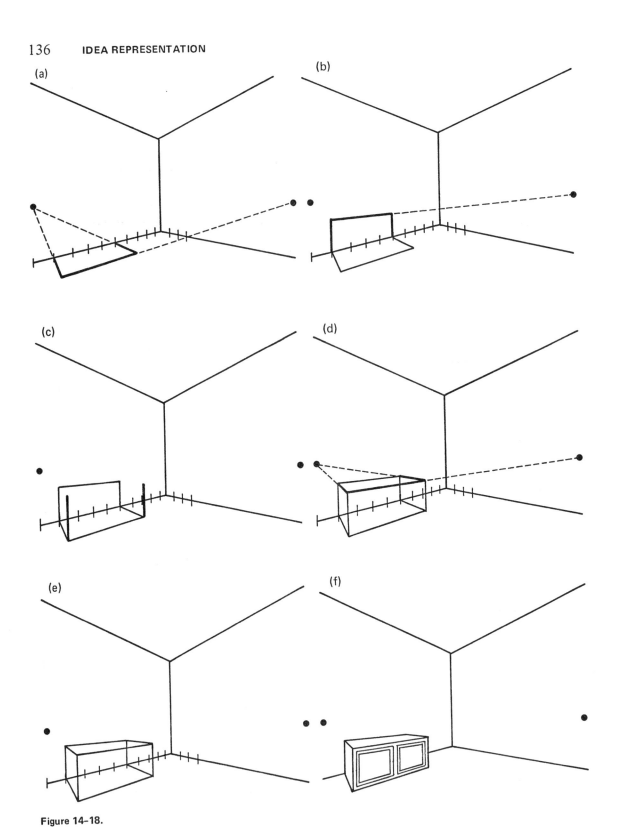

Figure 14–18.

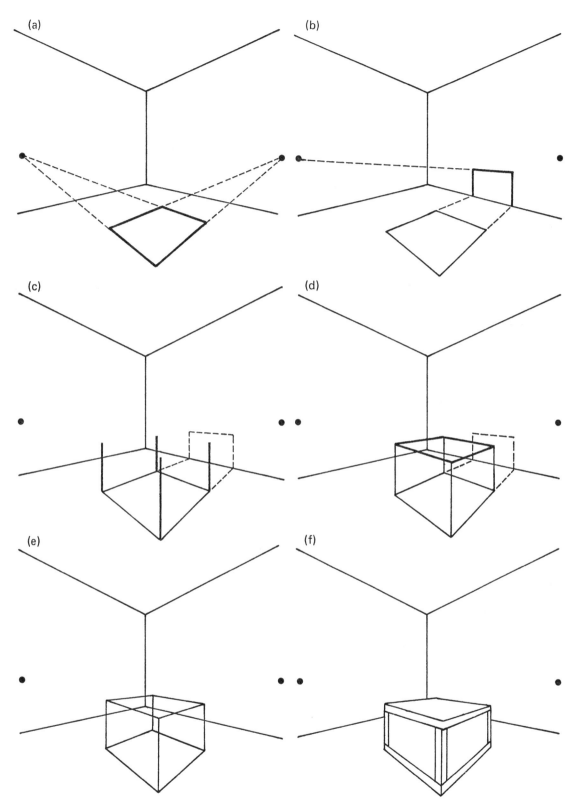

Figure 14–19.

14-19 shows how to draw a square or rectangular object that rests in the middle of the floor of a space but is placed squarely in the room. With one exception, these two objects are drawn exactly the same way.

The procedure for drawing an object that rests "irregularly" in a space, that is, one that doesn't parallel any wall, is shown in Figure 14-20. The only change in the original technique is that you move the two perspective points along the horizon line for *the same distance and in the same direction*. From this point on, you use the same technique to draw the object.

The same procedure is used to draw an irregularly placed object in a one-point perspective. In effect, you superimpose the two-point perspective on the one-point perspective to combine the drawings. You *must* use the same scale and horizon lines for the perspective points. Now look again at Figures 14-18–14-21 and study the different techniques.

HOW TO DRAW IN TWO-POINT PERSPECTIVE OBJECTS THAT APPEAR ON THE FLOOR OF A SPACE

When drawing objects that extend out into the room from a wall (with reference to Figure 14-18):

Figure 14–20.

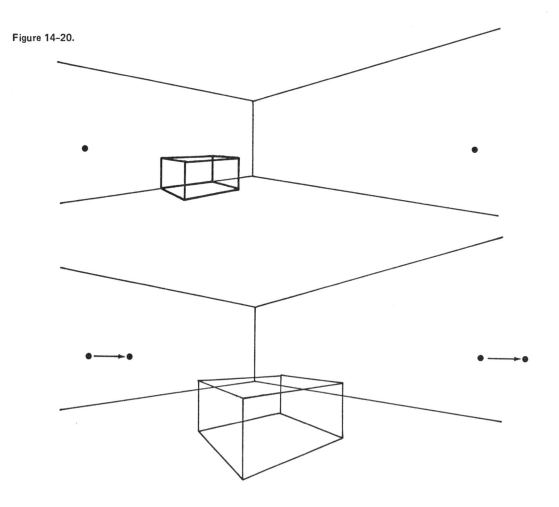

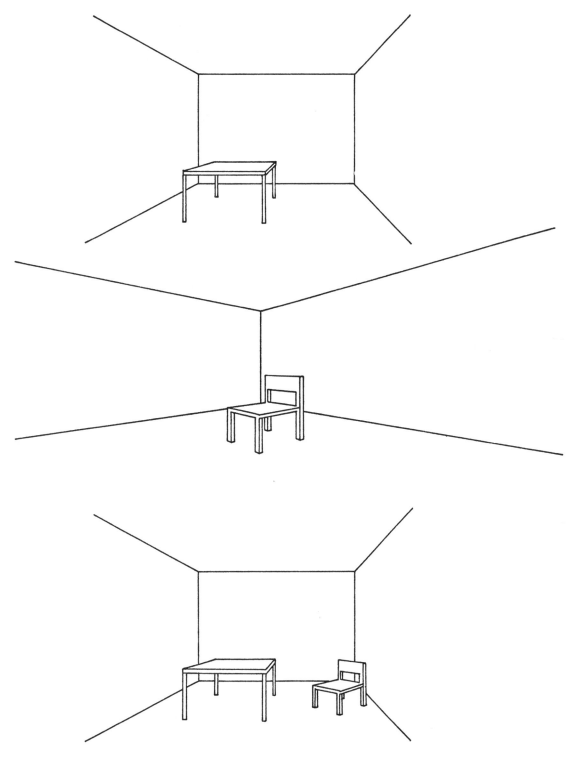

Figure 14-21.

1. Draw the space the object occupies on the floor. Do this by using both vanishing points and the foot marking that you have established. Erase all unnecessary lines as you proceed. (a)
2. Draw vertical lines from each corner where the "object" meets the wall. Then, using the appropriate vanishing point and height mark along the corner line, finish indicating the space that the object occupies on the wall. (b)

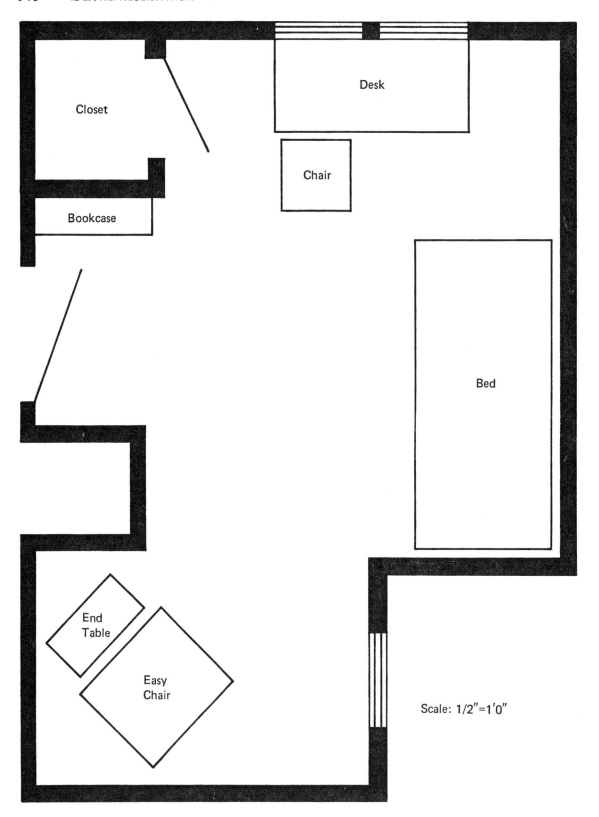

Closet

Desk

Chair

Bookcase

Bed

End Table

Easy Chair

Scale: 1/2″=1′0″

Figure 14–22.

3. Draw vertical lines from each front "corner." (c)
4. Using both vanishing points, draw the two top side lines and the top front line. (d)
5. (e) shows the resulting "box."
6. Add necessary detail. (f)

To draw in two-point perspective objects that appear on the floor of a space and are parallel to but not against a wall proceed exactly as you would in Figure 14-18, but *pretend* that the object really does rest against a wall. Draw the size of the object where it will lie in the space along with the distance that separates it from the nearest parallel wall. In effect, you will have an elongated object. When you have finished, erase the section that represents the space between the object and the wall. This area is shown in Figure 14-19 with broken lines (b, c, and d).

TASK DESCRIPTION AND TASK ANALYSIS

Task Description

Given all of the necessary architectural drawing equipment, you will be able to represent a specific space as a two-point perspective in scale.

Task Analysis

16 steps
1. Collect all necessary architectural drawing equipment.
2. Draw a floor plan of an existing or theoretical space, or refer to the floor plan that appears in Figure 14-22.
3. Select the two walls you want to illustrate.
4. Select a scale to work in.
5. Tape the drawing paper to the drafting surface with masking tape by placing a small piece of tape over each corner.
6. Measure the two walls and draw them on your drawing paper, as shown on the previous pages.
7. Draw the architectural details that appear on the walls, such as doors and windows.
8. Add wall details that are decorative, such as pictures.
9. "Box in" the furnishings that appear next to each wall.
10. "Box in" objects that are not against a wall but are parallel to one.
11. "Box in" objects that appear irregularly within the space.
12. Add detail to the walls and furnishings to make the space appear "lived in."
13. Add shadows and shading to the drawing to make it realistic.
14. Complete the title block in the corner with all the necessary information, as described earlier.
15. If you used a space other than the floor plan given in Figure 14-22, hand it in and indicate which walls you drew.
16. Hand the completed drawing to the instructor on the date assigned.

SUMMARY

"DRAWING" IT ALL TOGETHER AND GOING ONE STEP FURTHER

Now that we have completed all of the steps in the design process, a very important question remains: do you feel, at this point, that you could adequately have completed the later assignments concerned on spatial design independent of the preparatory knowledge about creativity, values, space, and methodology? If your answer to this question is "yes," then it is most important that you continue reading here. If you said "no," continue reading anyway, for you are on the author's preferred path. Both types of respondents gain insight into just why the book was arranged in the order that it was and presumably any remaining confusion will disappear.

The primary objective of this book was to emphasize the interrelationships between human behavior and the environment: they are inextricably linked and are interdependent. They exist because of each other and sometimes contradict each other. Several times, particularly when we discussed values and space, we studied these interrelationships and learned the necessity of having a working knowledge of human behavior before attempting spatial design. We have also seen that actually planning an architectural space before adequately analyzing the needs of the users can result in a totally inappropriate "solution." Once you have identified and satisfied the interrelationships and analyzed the entire problem with these determinants in mind, you can proceed with the synthesis aspect of the project. The dangers of a purely intuitive approach to problem solving you already know: take heed of them!

The direction taken in this book is an *ecological* one because of the interrelationship of humans and their environment. In the areas of interior design and housing, this relationship should be quite apparent. Let's look at an example, though, to see this relationship better. Let's see just how the environment can influence people in their life-styles and, in turn, how people can make decisions to influence the environment.

A family has moved to a new community three thousand miles from their former home. They are entirely unfamiliar with their new surroundings: they are aware that a vastly different climate will force some changes in their lives, but they are not very concerned about it. The purchase of some warm clothing will keep them warm in the winter, and the change from a predominance of air conditioning to heating will not be a great hardship, they decide. However, some new aspects of the family's future life have yet to become obvious to them. In their former residence, the power was generated hydroelectrically. Should they continue using all of the appliances that they brought with them (automatic clothes washer and dryer, frost-free refrigerator, trash compacter, and continuous-cleaning range), their new bills will be many times what they experienced before. Their independence in the past was due to their dependence upon such conveniences. They gave the family a certain amount of autonomy from the public services in their town, and now they have induced the family to purchase a home at a considerable distance from community services. It costs approximately the same to run their car now as it did before, but they are using it more often, and should they decide to utilize the commercial facilities, they will have to use the car even more frequently.

One good aspect of their move is the water situation: no more rationing! But their new home is in an area that requires imported fuel for home heating, and in the winter months their bills for this will amount to a great deal more than those they are used to receiving for air conditioning.

True, this example has been fabricated, but it is much like more than one family's experience. The home heating fuel, water, and electricity demands, along with the climate change, will have a definite impact upon the family's life-style. How will these conditions alter the family's life-style, or stated more ecologically, how will the environment affect the organisms (people) living within it and how will the organisms affect the environment in turn? A possibility would be to cut back on the consumption of electricity, if the people decided that they did not want to pay exorbitant electricity bills. This decision would mean lowering the household temperature, using appliances less often, and managing the household in ways conducive to less fossil fuel consumption and more human energy use. Thus there would probably have to be a greater allocation of family and individual time to doing chores by hand rather than by machine. Can you think of any ways this could be done?

A direct application to the housing industry in this case would be the development of smaller, energy-conserving residences. Also, the placement of the home on the land so that it can take maximum advantage of the sun's rays for warmth would contribute to the solution. The interior design industry would be included, for instance, through material selection that would save energy. The proper wall, floor, and window treatments for the season would have an effect upon energy savings, as would the appropriate education for their use and care. So the environment does affect the organisms, and the people, in order to survive, will interact with, and thus affect, the environment.

In the fields of interior design and housing, we are becoming more and more aware of the demands upon our industrial ingenuity than ever before. Because of our recent reminder that the earth's resources are finite, the industries that produce products for this field have had to develop ideas and materials consistent with a less energy-intensive society.

Now think back to the first unit of this book, where we talked about different elements of design theory. How can we relate design theory to ecology?

CREATIVITY

Remember that creativity is the art of coming up with new ideas. You learned how to develop new ideas primarily for interior spaces and small problems in Chapter 2. The same techniques can be used for larger problems. Today, more than at any other time, we must put our creative forces to work in dealing with environmental constraints. A good question to ask might be: how can we develop a more energy-efficient living environment without substantially disrupting out life-style or lowering our standard of living? This is a question that future interior designers and housing professionals must reckon with, because it will affect your livelihood and because you will be in a position to deal with it. The limited resources of the future demand that we utilize them more efficiently. An understanding of how to create the quality of life that individuals desire is going to increase in importance over the years, especially as we may have fewer and more expensive resources than we have now. For example, we will have less ground upon which to build, but more housing units to build for more people. How do you do it? You *create*, right? In this case, you cooperate and create with nature.

You will use creativity to develop both new products and new methods of obtaining acceptance for them. Why is the latter use important? For the answer, we have to proceed to the subject of values.

VALUES

As stated earlier, values can be rational or irrational. What really matters is that we realize that they determine how we act. For whatever reasons, people hold specific values and, therefore, act. Individuals with "new" or "better" ideas on how other people should act must deal with these values. Remember, values develop over time, and often over a long time. They do not change on a whim. We usually retain the basic values we learned as a child throughout life, and we are consciously or unconsciously sincere about them. They may alter, but their original integrity remains. Consequently, any attempt to change behavior, even for the betterment of the individual and society, must take note of the values of the individual and society.

Any decision, of course, depends upon a family's needs, goals, and desires. It also depends upon the family type. It is necessary that you, as a future environmental designer, be aware of this relationship since you may often come in contact with families, either directly or indirectly. In dealing with them, being able to discern the nature of the family will be indispensable in finding the proper approach to the solution of the problem.

For example, if the family in question here were a "closed" one, change might be impossible for them. Any necessary concessions to the new environment might have to be the result of necessity, such as exorbitantly high energy bills that it cannot afford, an absolute dearth of a certain product, or a law forbidding the product's use. In this case, a change might be mandatory, but the family really is not conditioned for it. As clients of yours, they could prove to be pretty difficult to deal with!

On the other hand, an "open" family would take a different point of view to problem solving. The well-being of the family members comes first. There are no absolute rules regarding the family's relationships to others and the environment. A positive outlook is inherent and flexibility is encouraged in all situations. When faced with a decision, the open family selects from among the various alternatives to find the most beneficial one. They seek constructive solutions that will enhance their lives. They have no hard and fast rules to observe. Change comes easy, and the family may be better adjusted to current living conditions because they would probably enter into them voluntarily and with a positive view. With all of these characteristics come creativity, inventiveness, spontaneity, and a certain amount of trust. Not that the closed family lacks these characteristics, but they seem to prevail more in open families. Which type do you think you would prefer working with?

Getting back to values and how they can affect decision making, consider the person who says she values economy. Because of this value, she habitually purchases the cheapest products available. She feels she is saving money this way. She is not very concerned if her purchases don't work properly and have to be replaced often. After all, she thinks, she didn't pay very much for them to begin with, and they can't be expected to last forever! If your job was to convince her to buy better-quality merchandise, how would you approach the problem? One way to do it would be to come right out and say, "If you would spend more money in the first place and buy a better product, you would be better off." But what would you be doing? You would be challenging her idea of "value." If she were to spend more money for the product, what would happen to her value of economy, in *her* perception?

A better way to attack the problem would be to emphasize the money-saving aspects of the more expensive product: it should last longer, work better, and not need frequent replacement. So, in the long run, the better, more expensive item may save money. By presenting the idea in the framework with which the individual is familiar, you would improve the chance that she would accept it because you would be respecting the original value.

From the ecological standpoint, many decisions of the future will involve questioning human values. Returning to the idea of the open and closed family concepts, you will find that the open family or person most likely will adapt values, if necessary, to resolve the problem at hand. As an example, let's say that A and B are both single-person households.

A has a very strong value of cleanliness and demands that the laundry be washed, dried, and stored properly every day. B basically has the same feeling towards cleanliness and, indeed, also has similar laundry habits. However, B decides that this practice is taking up too much time and is very costly in the monetary sense and chooses to do the laundry every third day. A says that doing the laundry every three days would violate the cleanliness value and would not do it, even though it does take time away from other activities that would be more pleasurable. B feels that the satisfaction of being able to participate in other activities compensates for the possible disturbance of seeing dirty laundry. Also, it takes less money to do the laundry because the washer and dryer are always full now when in use. Before, neither was ever full.

Which of the two is the "open" person here? In other words, who perceived a personal dissatisfaction, possible choices to improve it, and exercised ingenuity to devise a more satisfying life situation? B, of course. Right? In the design world, the tendency to be open to new ideas is called a "glass box" approach, as opposed to a "black box" one, which excludes new concepts.

We can use similar techniques when the environment has "told" us to change our lifestyles. When we no longer have adequate land to build a single-family, detached house for every family, how do we tell people that they will have to do without their lifelong dream, which a house still represents to most? Simply telling everyone to move into high-rise, efficiency apartments or condominiums will probably not work. How would *you* respond to that? Instead, once again we must research the values of the society and then respect them. Creating an environment that will satisfy the values, wants, and needs of its users will have to be done in conjunction with the users themselves. Trade-offs will be necessary, but eventually suitable solutions will be found.

SPACE

As population increases, physical space becomes a problem. Just how will the earth support its growing number of people? To put the problem in a more limited scope for now, how can we provide for people's needs for psychological, sociological, and physical space if our economy and natural resources dictate that we lessen the enclosed spatial allotments for people?

In response to this "suggestion" from the natural and man-made environments, interior design and housing students must continue to study the ways in which people and societies *use* space, how they *interpret* it, and what they *value* about it. Without such knowledge, housing alternatives such as condominiums and industrially built housing may never fulfill their potential. Often, they do not respect the individual space needs of people. People cannot relate to them or feel "at home" there.

Remember, we can analyze and provide for the actual physical-space needs of a family or individual but what about their need for safety, psychological stimulation, and creativity, among others? What if they aren't satisfied? Well, obviously the idea will have failed. Always keep in mind that a person's *perceived* situation is as good an indicator of his quality of life as his analytically evaluated situation is. Listen to what people say about their living environments. It is quite possible that their impressions will differ from yours, and their ideas may be more suited to the situation than yours are.

METHODOLOGY

Methodology was the last chapter in the first unit, and do you remember why? Because it is the vehicle for the complete, orderly investigation of a problem. Its use simplifies the problem-solving process. It allows you to view the relationships that have become apparent in the examination of space and values. It organizes your creativity and lets you be more creative.

Organization is especially important when the subject integrates several areas of knowledge. The ecological approach "naturally" integrates several areas. It does not separate subjects into distinct units. Rather, the ecological approach is a holistic one. Just think of how many seemingly divergent subjects the mention of interior design and housing imply: architecture, psychology, art, sociology, physiology . . . How many others? In order to make some sort of sense out of it, we must organize the subject matter.

That is what this book has been about: dissecting the design process. It illustrates that designing for people requires a considerable amount of research into the organisms themselves and their relation to the environment. It involves a sincere study of all the individual's environments: natural, social, psychological, and economic. All of these environments affect the individual, and in turn, the individual affects them.

Imagine that you are leaving today for a month-long camping trip in the mountains. Your goal is to "rough it," to test your ability to survive. You have taken just enough food for basic survival, a sleeping bag, a pup tent, one change of clothing, some matches, a lantern, and a radio (well, we're not all perfect, you know!). All right, where will you get water? From the nearby stream, eh? That's why you didn't bother bringing any with you, you say? The environment influenced you before you even left home, didn't it? You *interacted* with it. You knew that water was there, and you planned to use it. For cooking and your personal warmth, how will you cooperate with nature? Surely you can't stay bundled up in your sleeping bag all month! Oh, wood has generously been provided by the forest you are visiting? By burning wood, you make a reciprocal impact upon the land: you diminish the amount of wood in the area, you cause pollution, and you may help beautify and make the woods a healthier place for other plants if you are careful and burn only wood that is dead or has fallen to the ground. You also can collect food to supplement your supply of dried beef. The list of reciprocal relationships could go on and on. Do you see it?

The point of this story is that we exist with nature, whether we are in the woods, as depicted here, or in a plush, lush, metropolitan suburb. We exist with nature and it exists with us. Together our actions and reactions form a system that sustains itself and continues sustaining itself until one element oversteps its bounds and throws the system out of balance. This is how the ecological approach works and how it explains the true *nature* of interior design and housing.

WORKSHEETS

Name _____

Have you ever been in this physical space before? _____ Whether you have or not, write your impressions of this physical space below. Be as descriptive and truthful as possible. Write down everything you can recall. Some key words are listed below to help your memory.

building exterior _____

_____

_____

building entrance and stairwell/staircase_____

_____

_____

windows, walls, ceilings, floors_____

_____

_____

furnishings, lighting _____

_____

_____

anything else?_____

_____

_____

Name _____

SPACE PLANNING

Today you are asked to plan a residence hall room for a typical student whom we'll call Pat. Since Pat is very normal as far as students go, the room will be used for studying, sleeping, visiting with friends, reading, and other assorted activities.

The space you have to work with appears on the reverse side of this page. You can do anything you want to it. Keep in mind how normal Pat is.

You are to do this exercise with someone else. One person will solve the problem while the other records all of the steps. Then, after the problem has been solved, the two of you can select the materials you would like to see used in this space. Attach the materials to this paper, and be sure to label what sample is to be used for what.

The last part of this project is to list any kind of additional information you feel would have helped you in solving this problem. If you feel the information given was adequate, say so.

You have a time limit of one classroom period in which to do this work.

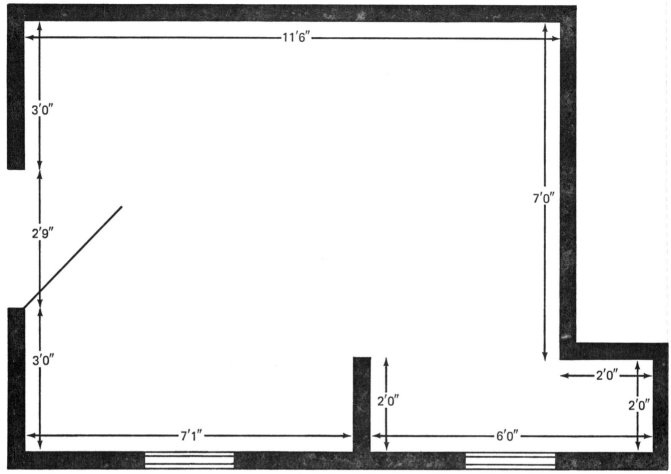

Scale: 1/2″ = 1′0″

Name _____

PSYCHOLOGICAL BLOCKS

Answer questions 1 and 2 below, and then answer question 3 as completely and imaginatively as possible. Keep the systems approach in mind.

1. Have you solved the problem? _____
2. Taking a hint from the reading, what was the problem?
    a. You are a professional bear catcher who was behind in your quota, and you had to catch up fast.
    b. You had to catch as many bears as possible.
    c. You had to get rid of the bears.
3. How else could the problem really have been solved? _____

_____

_____

_____

_____

_____

_____

_____

_____

_____

_____

_____

Name _____

DESCRIPTION BY ASSOCIATION

In the spaces below, name five familiar objects and "describe them by association." Then, sketch what you have described to see how accurate your verbal "picture" is.

1. _____   _____

   Sketch: _____

2. _____   _____

   Sketch: _____

3. _____   _____

   Sketch: _____

4. _____   _____

   Sketch: _____

5. _____   _____

   Sketch: _____

Name _____

RANK ORDERING

Rank the following alternatives 1 (your first choice), 2 (your second choice), 3 (your third choice), or 4 (your fourth choice).

1. Where would you choose to live?
   - _____ In an urban center
   - _____ In a suburb of a large city
   - _____ In a rural area

2. What feature of a house would you choose to be the most important?
   - _____ Low monthly payments
   - _____ Comfort
   - _____ Prestige
   - _____ Beauty

3. What do you consider most important in a neighborhood?
   - _____ Friendly neighbors
   - _____ Quiet
   - _____ Expensive houses
   - _____ Your own home

4. What would you prefer to live in?
   - _____ A high-rise apartment building
   - _____ A low-rise apartment or condominium
   - _____ A single-family detached house

5. What do you consider most important in design?
   - _____ Pleasing people, no matter what that entails
   - _____ Doing the job correctly, as you feel it should be
   - _____ Doing whatever will cost people most

6. You have $2000 to spend on furniture for your first apartment. Will you:
   - _____ Spend it all on one famous chair that you have always wanted
   - _____ Spend it all on a few pieces of good-quality furniture
   - _____ Spend it all on low-quality furniture in order to fill the entire space

7. What do you value most?
   - _____ A large, airy apartment
   - _____ Good neighbors and friends nearby
   - _____ A pleasant neighborhood

8. What could you give up if you had to?

_____ Your individual home

_____ Your accustomed purchasing power

_____ Your free time

9. You now have a job and can afford to support yourself. What will you do?

_____ Continue to live with your parents

_____ Find an apartment near your parents

_____ Move completely across town so that you don't see your family every day

10. What would you look for first in a community when selecting a home?

_____ Closeness to shopping facilities (food, clothing, miscellaneous)

_____ Closeness to entertainment facilities (movies, sports, nightclubs, restaurants)

_____ Closeness to outdoor recreational facilities (parks, playgrounds)

11. You have just gotten a job working in a large business firm. What would you like?

_____ Your own office down the hall and away from everyone

_____ An office area in a large room with other people who are similarly employed

_____ A small office of your own close to other people who are similarly employed

Name _____

YOU, THE CONSUMER

You have just inherited 4700 record albums from your Great Uncle Clyde, who has found greater joy in cassettes. Surprisingly, you discover that there are some "classics" that you would like to hear, but you have nothing to play them on. You decide to purchase *something* to play them on. What will you do? Answer the following questions, telling what you will do ("action"), why you will do it ("why?"), and what value you feel by your thoughts and actions illustrate ("value").

	Action	*Why?*	*Value*
1. What will you buy?			
2. Where will you buy it?			
3. How much will you spend?			
4. Where will you put it?			

Name _____

YOU, THE DISASTER VICTIM

You have just heard that you have five minutes to get yourself and everything you can out of your habitat before it is destroyed by a rampaging brush fire. What five items will you take? List below the objects you will save and explain why you chose them.

1.

2.

3.

4.

5.

Name _____

LIVING ENVIRONMENT PREFERENCES

Find two pictures of living spaces, exterior or interior, that you would (1) enjoy living in or (2) detest living in. Attach them below in the appropriate spaces and tell why you would either enjoy or detest living there. Then identify your values as you have alluded to them.

1. Enjoy   2. Detest

1. Why?   2. Why?

Name _____

SIGNIFICANT ENVIRONMENTS

Describe in detail two environments that have influenced you significantly. The first one should be a space that you feel was designed for your comfort because the provider actually cared about you. For the second one, choose a space that you feel is basically hostile: it seems that the provider cared little, if at all, for your comfort, and cared only about function. Also tell why you chose these places and why you feel they affected you as they did.

1. Sensitive environment:

2. Insensitive environment:

Name _____

ANTHROPOMETRICS I

Select an object you would like to custom design for yourself. It can be anything: an article of clothing, a piece of furniture, a gadget you want. Just choose something that you will physically come in contact with. Name the object here: _____.

What function is it to perform? _____

_____

In the space below, sketch the part of you that will be critical to your object. For example, if you are designing a pair of gloves, draw your hand and wrist. Measure that part of you with a ruler, draw it, and record the proper measurements.

Finally, sketch your object as accurately as possible. Include all necessary measurements that you have used as the basis of your design.

Name _____

ANTHROPOMETRICS II

List ten items that you believe were designed anthropometrically and tell why you chose these items.

1. _____ Why? _____

_____

2. _____ Why? _____

_____

3. _____ Why? _____

_____

4. _____ Why? _____

_____

5. _____ Why? _____

_____

6. _____ Why? _____

_____

7. _____ Why? _____

_____

8. _____ Why? _____

_____

9. _____ Why? _____

_____

10. _____ Why? _____

_____

Name _____

PHYSICAL, PSYCHOLOGICAL, AND SOCIAL SPACE

I. Match the following:
   a. Physical space   _____The view a window provides from a small space

   b. Psychological space   _____Space in a kitchen work zone

   c. Social space   _____A lounge in a residence hall

                              _____Space between chairs for conversation

                              _____Space allowed for clothing in a room

                              _____Room for furniture dimensions

                              _____Space for an individual to feel comfortable

                              _____The balcony of an apartment

                              _____A bench for adults near a playground

II. Define the following in your own words:
   a. Physical space: _____

   _____

   b. Psychological space: _____

   _____

   c. Social space: _____

   _____

Name _____

PERSONAL SPACE AND TERRITORIALITY

In your own words, define the following terms:

1. Personal space: _____

   _____

   _____

   _____

2. Territoriality: _____

   _____

   _____

   _____

3. Personalization: _____

   _____

   _____

   _____

4. Privacy: _____

   _____

   _____

   _____

5. Recall a time when you felt "lost," for example, when you had no place you felt was really your own. What happened? How did you feel? What did you do? _____

_____

_____

_____

_____

_____

_____

6. Recall a time when you felt threatened in a place that was your own. What happened? How did you feel? What did you do? _____

_____

_____

_____

_____

_____

_____

Name _____

SIDEWALK SPACE

This is a problem you will do on a sidewalk. On a pleasant day, seek out ten "victims." Be very careful that they fit the following criteria:

a. They are alone.
b. They are walking on the right side of the sidewalk.
c. They are not carrying any large or bulky objects that would impede their movement.

Then approach your "victim" head on on the left side of the sidewalk. Five times record what happens to you and your subject when you approach him or her looking straight ahead, apparently paying attention to what you are doing. Record your action and the reaction of the subject. Approach the next five victims the same way, but make it appear that you are not paying attention to what you are doing. Record your action and your subject's reaction.

Paying Attention to What You Are Doing

1. Your action: _____

   Victim's reaction: _____

   _____

2. Your action: _____

   Victim's reaction: _____

   _____

3. Your action: _____

   Victim's reaction: _____

   _____

4. Your action: _____

   Victim's reaction: _____

   _____

5. Your action: _____

   Victim's reaction: _____

   _____

Not Paying Attention to What You Are Doing

1. Your action: _____

   Victim's reaction: _____

   _____

2. Your action: _____

   Victim's reaction: _____

   _____

3. Your action: _____

   Victim's reaction: _____

   _____

4. Your action: _____

   Victim's reaction: _____

   _____

5. Your action: _____

   Victim's reaction: _____

   _____

Name _____

RELATING SPATIAL CONCEPTS TO FLOOR PLANS

As you will see, a floor plan is the graphic representation of any design concept including physical, psychological, and social space, along with value judgments, privacy, control, and other human considerations.

On the following pages, two outlines of rooms appear. One is an office, the other a living/dining space similar to that found in many homes today. Your job is to arrange furnishings within the space to facilitate the use of that space as described on the project sheet. Use the templates provided for you to place the furnishings. Choose the proper scale, cut out the templates, place them where you want them in the space, and glue them to the project sheet or trace around them. A few pointers to remember:

1. People need *at least* two feet between objects in order to move through the space. Leave *at least* this much space where you expect even minimal traffic.
2. Allow two or three inches between movable furnishings and walls. Built-ins should be flush against the walls.

After you have arranged the spaces, record how you satisfied the human needs for physical, psychological, and social space. Be specific in your answers, and refer to the text when necessary.

Office Plan Arrangement

Use: A lawyer requires a space that includes a personal work surface that is easily accessible to reference material, extra seating for visitors and clients, and a work surface for a small group. This surface may be incorporated in the personal work surface, if necessary.

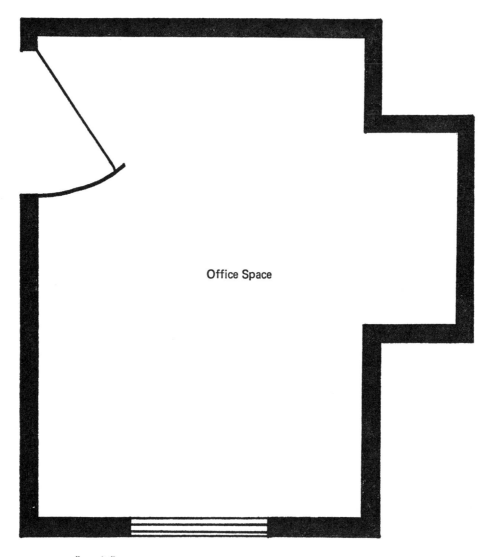

Office Space

Scale: 1/2″ = 1′0″

Explain how you have satisfied the human needs for

1. Physical space: _____

   _____

   _____

2. Psychological space: _____

   _____

   _____

3. Social space: _____

   _____

   _____

Living/Dining Plan Arrangement

Use: A family of four requires seating, eating, lounging, and miscellaneous living space where the entire family can gather together.

FIGURE HERE

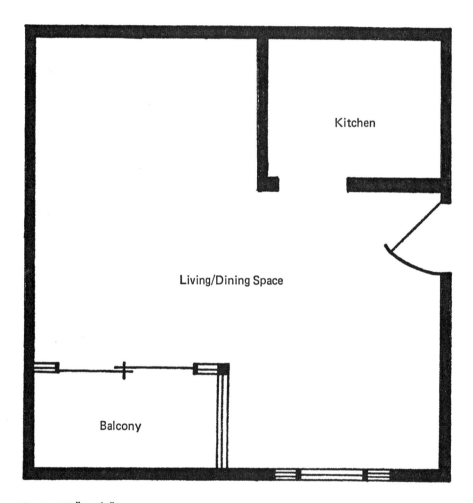

Scale: 1/4″ = 1′0″

Explain how you have satisfied the human needs for

1. Physical space: _____

   _____

   _____

2. Psychological space: _____

   _____

   _____

3. Social space: _____

   _____

   _____

Furniture Templates

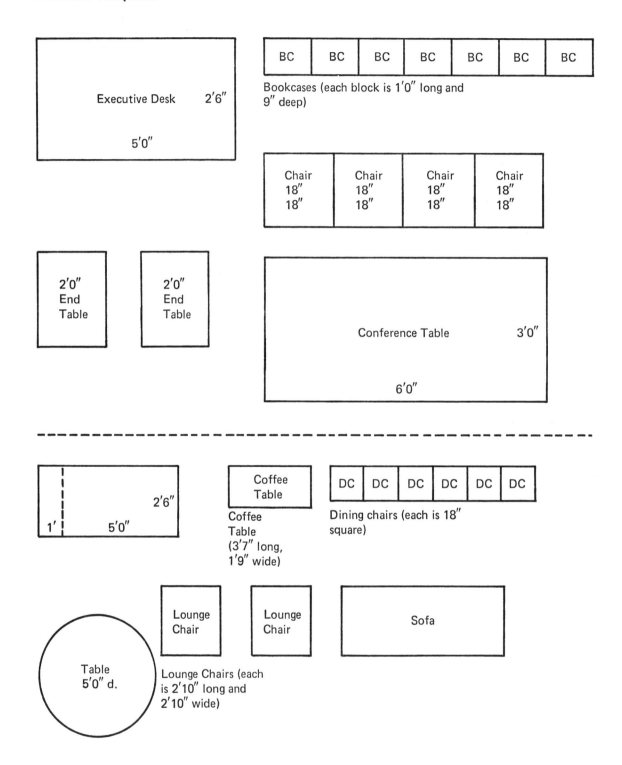

Name _____

Read and complete the following according to the guidance given in Chapter 5. Your problem is to design your own living space. Create your own "information" based on a project you have done or are thinking about. Then construct partial and combined solutions in the spaces indicated.

Problem: The design of your own space for living.
Information

1. _____

2. _____

3. _____

4. _____

5. _____

6. _____

Analysis

   1. Partial solutions

     a. _____

       _____

     b. _____

       _____

     c. _____

       _____

2. Combined solutions

   a. _____

   _____

   _____

   _____

   _____

Name _____

CREATING A METHOD

At some time or another, you have created a method for yourself so that you could complete a project effectively. Now think of a task that you perform regularly. It may be anything: a household chore, a hobby technique, an athletic effort, or the repair of an object, to name a few. Name the task you chose on the appropriate line below and then describe the activity by answering the four questions in part 2. In part 3 detail how you accomplish that task, step by step. Be sure to list *everything*. List only one action for each letter. Use an extra sheet of paper to complete your list, if necessary.

1. Task: _____
2. Task description:
   a. Audience (who will do it?) _____

   b. Behavior (what will be done?) _____

   c. Conditions (under what conditions will it be done?) _____

   _____

   d. Degree (what standards should be met?) _____

   _____
3. Task analysis:

   a. _____

   b. _____

   c. _____

   d. _____

   e. _____

   f. _____

   g. _____

h. _____

i. _____

j. _____

k. _____

l. _____

m. _____

n. _____

o. _____

p. _____

q. _____

r. _____

s. _____

t. _____

u. _____

v. _____

w. _____

Name _____

YOUR OWN DESIGN

Design an object for someone else's use, preferably a child's or an elderly person's. Solve the problem methodically. Fill in the blanks on this sheet according to the text descriptions of each step in the design process. Use additional paper and attach it to this sheet for the information, analysis, synthesis, and evaluation portions of this project.

1. Prestatement (in this case, what, in general, do you hope to do?): _____

   _____

   _____

   _____

2. Problem statement: _____

   _____

   _____

   _____

On a separate sheet of paper write down (3) the information, (4) analysis, (5) synthesis, and (6) evaluation.

Name _____

1. What three purposes do schematic drawings serve?

   a. _____

   b. _____

   c. _____

2. What is a bubble diagram? Select and circle the letter that precedes the appropriate answer.
   a. A diagram showing how to blow a bubble
   b. A diagram showing what a properly blown bubble should look like
   c. A schematic drawing

3. Why is it necessary to use the word "relative" instead of "actual" when discussing schematic drawings? _____
   _____

4. Organize the following list of activities into a schematic drawing. First indicate which activities are related and then sketch the appropriate bubble diagram.
   a. Sleeping
   b. Dressing
   c. Cooking
   d. Physical maintenance
   e. Clothing storage
   f. Entertaining
   g. Eating
   h. Outdoor recreation
   i. Playing quiet games

Name _____

For the list of activities given in Chapter 6 devise an alternative series of relationships. Indicate the new relationships with lines, as you were shown, and then sketch the new schematic drawing below.

Activities   *Schematic Drawing*

1. Reading
2. Writing
3. Studying
4. Sleeping
5. Book storage
6. Clothing storage
7. Talking to friends
8. Watching TV

Name _____

WORKING WITH A CLIENT

You are now going to make up a schematic drawing from what your client has told you she needs. Read the client's statement, determine what her needs are, and list them. Indicate the activity relationships, and then make your schematic drawing.

Client: "I really have a problem. I like to do a lot of crafts, but never have a decent place in which to do them. I macrame, so I need someplace to put projects that I am making as wall hangings. Also, sometimes I make things that will be suspended from the ceiling, such as planters, lamps, and hanging tables. Do you have any idea how difficult it is to work on something like this while it is hanging on a doorknob? Take my word—it's nearly impossible! You can drown in your string if you're not careful. Anyway, I découpage, too, and need a large work surface for this. Oh, for my rug hooking and macrame, I need a place to dye string. Storage is a big problem. All my beads, rope, string, nuts, bones, wood, yarn, varnish, pens, scissors, tape . . . oh, and my reference books! Also, finished products—I never know what to do with them! They usually end up on the floor in a box and get all dirty. Well, good luck—and I hope you can get this done for me in a week!"*

Needs   *Schematic Drawing*

*The author's thanks to Tara McPeek.

Name _____

TASK DESCRIPTION/TASK ANALYSIS

Task Description

Draw a schematic drawing that can be used in a formal design presentation, according to the standards discussed in class.

Task Analysis (9 steps)

1. List activities that you would like to be able to do in a particular place in your home. They might relate to work, hobby activities, and so on.
2. Indicate the relationships between activities with lines, as illustrated in the text.
3. Collect a pencil, scratch paper, a piece of 9 X 12-inch poster board, a black ink pen or thin-tip felt marker, and several variously colored wide-tip felt markers.
4. Following the steps mentioned in the schematic drawing section, sketch a preliminary bubble diagram on scratch paper.
5. Very lightly, in pencil, sketch the schematic drawing on the poster board, placing it so that the proportions of the drawing are appropriate for the size of the board. Make sure the drawing will be large enough to be seen and read from a distance of four to five feet.
6. Go over the pencil lines of the bubbles with ink. Make your lines dark and sure so that they can be seen from a distance of four to five feet.
7. Color each bubble differently. Use primary colors for major activities as much as possible so that they will produce secondary colors when the bubbles overlap.
8. Label the drawing completely. Note what each bubble stands for by lettering the name of the activity in the bubble. Be sure that all your lettering is neat, legible, and uniform in size and style. Use guidelines or a prepared, purchased, press-on type lettering (see Chapter 8).
9. Hand in the list of activities, preliminary sketch, and finished drawing on the assigned date.

Name _____

1. Draw a line representing *five feet, nine inches* in:
   a. One-inch scale
   b. Half-inch scale
   c. Quarter-inch scale
   d. One-eighth-inch scale
2. Draw a line representing *twelve feet, six inches* in:
   a. Three-eighths-inch scale
   b. Half-inch scale
   c. One-eighth-inch scale
   d. Quarter-inch scale
3. Using the dimensions in the diagram below, draw the correct figure in $\frac{1}{4}$″ scale.

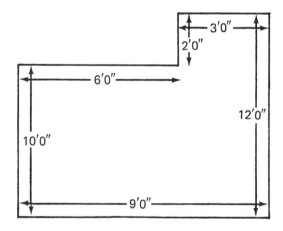

4. What does $\frac{1}{4}$″ = 1′0″ mean?
5. What purpose does an architect's scale serve? Why do we use it in design?

Name _____

The figures that follow are in quarter-inch, half-inch, or one-inch scale. Draw the figures in the other two scales.

Example:

$\frac{1}{4}'' = 1'0''$ $\frac{1}{2}'' = 1'0''$ $1'' = 1'0''$

Given:

Draw:

1.

2.

WORKSHEET 24

¼″ = 1′0″   ½″ = 1′0″   1″ = 1′0″

3.

4.

5.

6.

7.

8.

9.

10.

Name _____

The following rough sketches contain measurements indicating the size of the rooms represented. Draw the "rooms" in quarter-inch scale.

1.

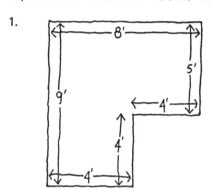

2.

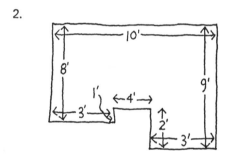

3.

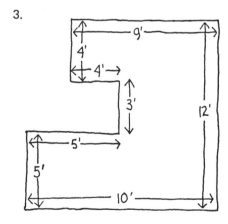

Name _____

Using a T square or parallel bar, triangle, and standard ruler, architecturally draft the following shapes. The rough sketches and their measurements are your guides. Draw your version in the space to the right of the sketch.

1.

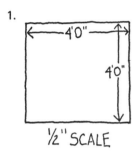

½" SCALE

2.

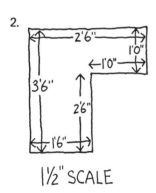

1½" SCALE

3.

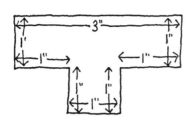

4.

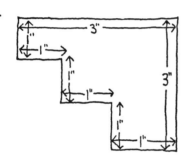

5.

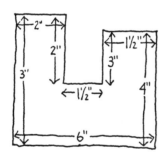

Name _____

Using a T square or parallel bar, triangle, and architect's scale, architecturally draft the following shapes. The rough sketches and their measurements are your guides. Draw your version in the space to the right of the sketch. Note the scale for each sketch and illustrate it appropriately.

1.

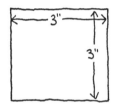

2.

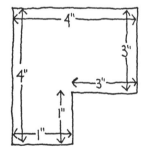

3.

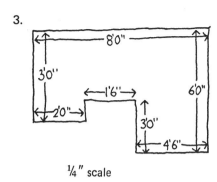

¼" scale

4.

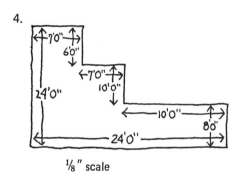

⅛" scale

5.

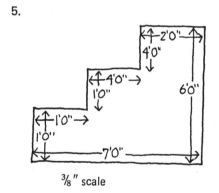

⅜" scale

Name _____

This time you are on your own! Select a space, measure it, and architecturally draw it in quarter-inch scale. Make a rough sketch of the space and record the measurements. Then draft a scale drawing.

Rough sketch with measurements:

Drafted sketch:

Name —————————————————

DIFFERENT CONNOTATIONS OF LETTERING

Find ten different kinds of lettering. Look in periodicals, newspapers, menus, pamphlets, and so on. Tape the samples to this sheet, then tell where you found it and what it was used for. Next, give an example of another use for this type of lettering.

Name _____

Practice the lettering below on the lines provided. Also practice on $\frac{1}{4}''$ graph paper and attach it to this sheet when you hand it in.

A	S
B	T
C	U
D	V
E	W
F	X
G	Y
H	Z
I	1
J	2
K	3
L	4
M	5
N	6
O	7
P	8
Q	9
R	0

Name _____

Practice the lettering below on the lines that have been provided. Also, practice additionally on $\frac{1}{4}''$ graph paper and attach it to this sheet when you hand it in.

A	S
B	T
C	U
D	V
E	W
F	X
G	Y
H	Z
I	1
J	2
K	3
L	4
M	5
N	6
O	7
P	8
Q	9
R	0

Name _____

Practice the lettering below on the lines provided. Also practice on $\frac{1}{4}''$ graph paper and attach it to this sheet when you hand it in.

a   a
b   b
c   c
d   d
e   e
f   f
g   g
h   h
i   i
j   j
k   k
l   l
m   m
n   n
o   o
p   p
q   q
r   r
s   s
t   t
u   u
v   v
w   w
x   x
y   y
z   z

Name _____

The house below is drawn in eighth-inch scale. Your job is to *label* the areas as you believe they might be in life. Using your knowledge of human behavior and how it can affect spatial layout, decide for yourself what space is going to be used for what. Also use your best lettering. Label this drawing completely and explain why you identified the spaces as you did.

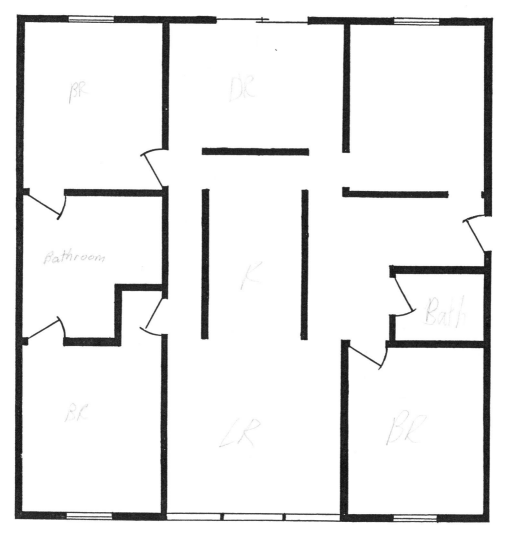

Name _____

The space below has been drawn for you in ¼″ scale. Your job is to *dimension* it thoroughly. Add the dimension lines with breaks for measurements. If an object exceeds more than one foot in length, indicate the measurement in both feet and inches. This instruction applies even if the object measures exactly in feet without extra inches.

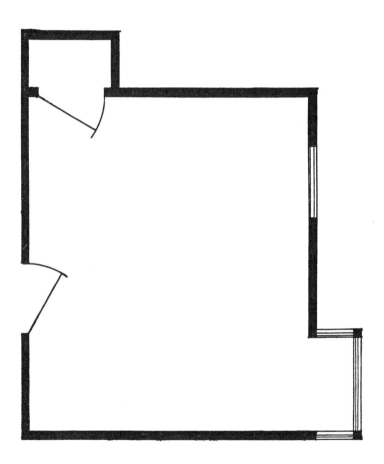

Name _____

This time you are on your own. Select a space, and measure it. Then, using your drafting equipment, draw it in the space below. Choose a relatively small space, one that does not exceed 14'0'' X 16'0''. Draw the space in half-inch scale and label and dimension it fully.

Name _____

Illustrate how to determine the shape of a space from the activities that it will support. A list of activities has been provided. You are to: (1) draw a bubble diagram of the activities; (2) indicate the furnishings that might be representative of the activities; and (3) illustrate a feasible spatial shape. Include door and window placement. Do not architecturally draft this space; stop short of that.

Activities:

1. Canned goods storage
2. Boxed goods storage
3. Baking and mixing of foods
4. Eating space for two
5. Sewing
6. Washing and drying dishes
7. Plants
8. Plant material storage (pots, soil, etc.)
9. Refrigeration

Name _____

1. What dimensions does a floor plan show? _____

   and _____ .

2. What is the primary function of a floor plan? _____

   _____

3. What three aspects of space influence a floor plan and the placement of objects within it?

   _____ , _____ and

   _____ .

4. Why are architectural symbols used on floor plans? _____

   _____

   _____

5. Identify in the spaces provided the architectural symbols pictured here.

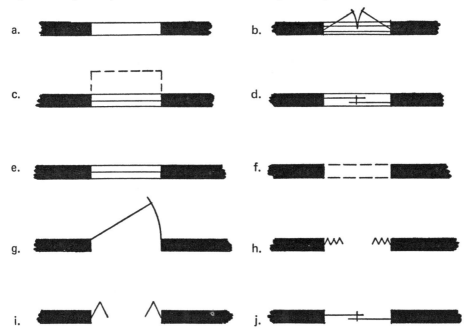

a.   b.

c.   d.

e.   f.

g.   h.

i.   j.

Name _____

This space has been outlined in *quarter-inch* scale. Finish the drawing by selecting and adding doors and windows; indicate the location of each with the appropriate architectural symbol. Following that, label the space by *dimensioning it* (see Figure 9-17). Decide what type of space it is by analyzing its size and shape. The only constraints are the "door" indicated by the break in the wall and the "windows," which are the open spaces in the darkened wall sections.

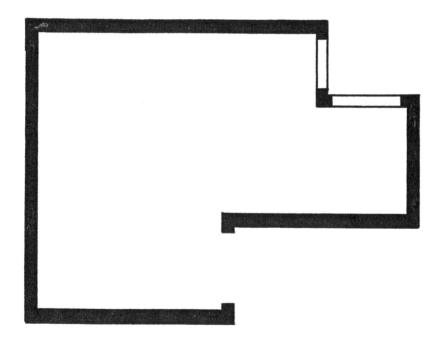

Name _____

The space on the reverse side of this page has been outlined in half-inch scale. Finish the drawing by adding doors and windows. Mark them with appropriate architectural symbols. Then fill in the walls. Following that, label the space to show *its furnishings*, as done in Figure 9-18. Decide what type of space it is by analyzing its size and shape. The only constraint is the door, which is symbolized by the break in the wall. Work with this constraint.

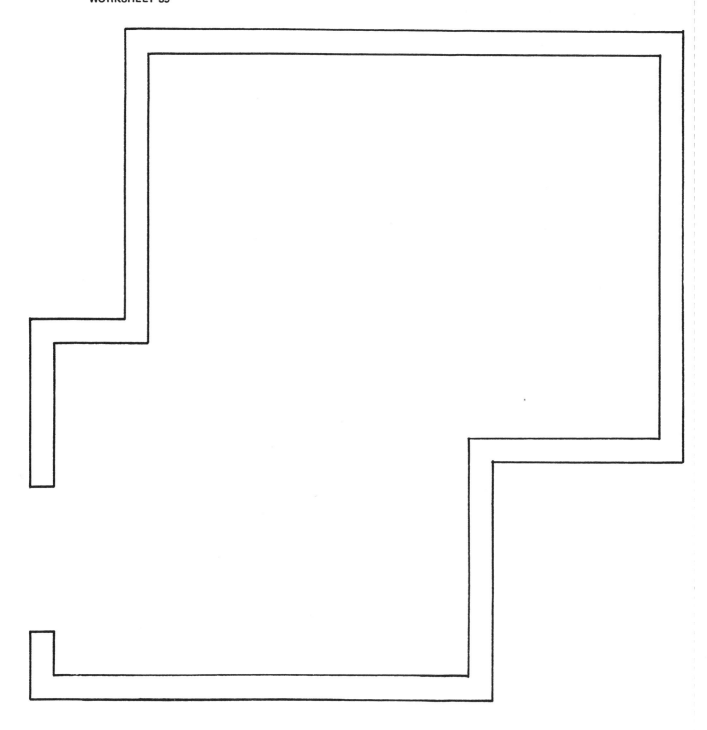

Name _____

The following problem asks you to design this space for a client with whom you are already familiar. Worksheet 21 includes a statement specifying what this person needs in her work space. Repeating her statement here should refresh your memory.

I really have a problem. I like to do a lot of crafts, but never have a decent place in which to do them. I macrame, so I need someplace to put projects that I am making as wall hangings. Also, sometimes I make things that will be suspended from the ceiling, such as planters, lamps, and hanging tables. Do you have any idea how difficult it is to work on something like this while it is hanging on a doorknob? Take my word—it's nearly impossible! You can drown in your string if you're not careful. Anyway, I découpage, too, and need a large work surface for this. Oh, for my rug hooking and macrame, I need a place to dye string. Storage is a big problem. All my beads, rope, string, nuts, bones, wood, yarn, varnish, pens, scissors, tape . . . oh, and my reference books! Also, finished products—I never know what to do with them! They usually end up on the floor in a box and get all dirty. Well, good luck—and I hope you can get this done for me in a week!

For that project you drew up a list of needs and a schematic drawing for this person. Refer back to them now and use them as a background for your floor plan. Follow the task description and task analysis guidelines given in Chapter 9 in drafting this space.

Name _____

Create a drawing from your own specifically outlined needs. Make a list of activities for the space, develop a schematic drawing, then follow the task description and task analysis guidelines given in Chapter 9 to complete a floor-plan drawing. Quarter- or half-inch scale is acceptable. Label the drawing by showing its furnishings, as indicated in Figure 9-18.

Name _____

1. Why would you use an elevation drawing in a design presentation? _____

_____

_____

2. What relationship does an elevation have to a floor plan in a total design presentation? Check one:

_____ It replaces it

_____ It complements it

3. With regard to your answer in number 2, defend your choice. _____

_____

_____

4. What does an elevation *not* show? Name at least three items.

   a. _____

   b. _____

   c. _____

5. Indicate which walls would appear on an elevation in the floor plans on the reverse side of this page, assuming you are to draw the "south" wall. Draw a line along the entire wall to show your choice.

N

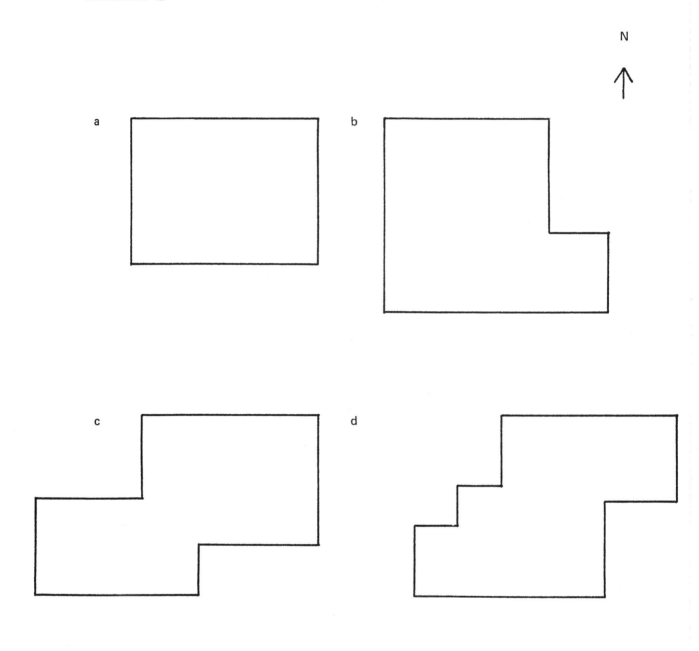

a

b

c

d

Name _____

Finish the following elevation by adding any detail you feel is necessary. Indicate materials, finishes, and add personal touches; in other words, make the drawing as realistic as possible. Refer to Figure 9-11 for hints.

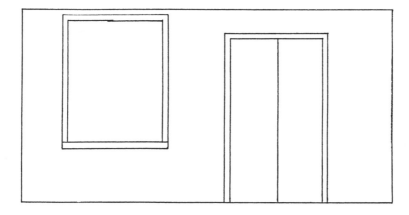

Name _____

Utilizing the floor plan below, draw an elevation for each wall in $\frac{1}{4}$'' scale. Include all detail necessary to make the space real.

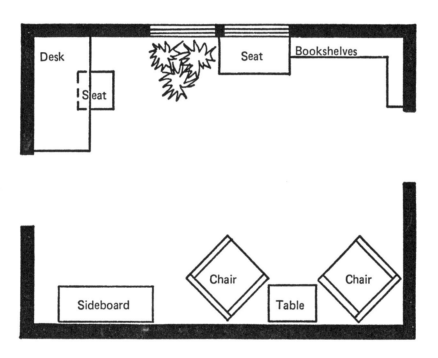

Name _____

Upholstered Chair —

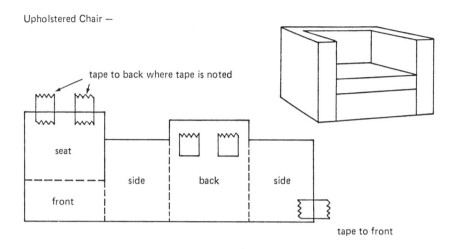

tape to back where tape is noted

seat

front

side

back

side

tape to front

Upholstered Sofa —

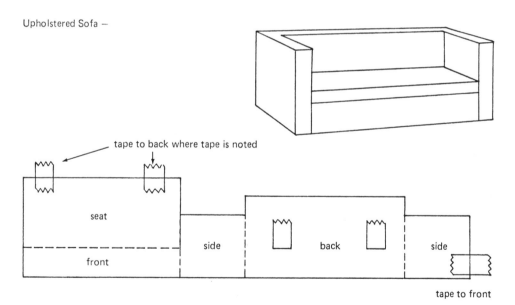

tape to back where tape is noted

seat

front

side

back

side

tape to front

Cut on solid lines; fold on dotted lines. Tape where noted.

Upholstery. Using the patterns above cut the upholstery by allowing twice the fabric the patterns indicate. For example, the chair upholstery would be cut as follows:

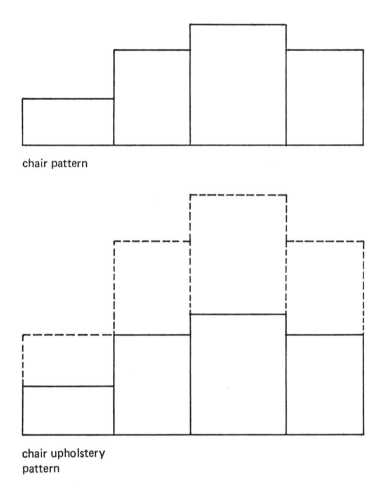

chair pattern

chair upholstery
pattern

Then glue the fabric to the outside chair base, fold the fabric *over the top* of the base, and glue again at the inside bottom.

Next, refold the furniture along the lines previously established (by the dotted lines), and secure where noted with tape or glue. (Sometimes, with fabric, taping first, then gluing is necessary when taping alone will not hold. When the glue has dried, remove the tape. Using a clear glue generously on the wrong side of the piece works best.)

Use the same technique for sofas and other furniture that you develop.

Furniture that is not upholstered is easier to make, of course. Simply measure what you want to make, draw it in scale, cut it out, tape or glue it together, and finish it how you like.

Name _____

Create an elevation drawing from your own, specifically outlined needs. Refer to the floor plan that you created for Worksheet 41, select a detailed wall, and then follow the task description and task analysis provided in Chapter 10 to complete an elevation. You may use quarter- or half-inch scale. No labeling is necessary since the inclusion of material symbols will identify the objects.

Name _____

1. Finish drawing the boxes below in perspective. Make them all appear to be the same size as those that have been started for you.

2. How many boxes are now drawn in perspective? _____

3. If the vanishing point is directly below a box, what part(s) of the box will be visible? ____

   _____

4. If the vanishing point is above and to the right of a box, what part(s) of the box will be visible? _____

5. If the vanishing point is below and to the left of a box, what part(s) of the box will be visible? _____

6. If the vanishing point is directly behind the box, what part(s) of the box will be visible?

   _____

Name _____

Draw the "spaces" below, according to the instructions given. First, place the vanishing point. Then draw in the wall lines from the corner of the space out only. See the example:

Example: Show more of the left wall.

Given: You draw:

1. Show more of the right wall.

2. Show more of the ceiling.

3. Show more of the floor.

Name _____

Draw the "spaces" below, according to the instructions given. First, place the vanishing points. Then extend the wall lines from the top and bottom of the corner line of the space.

Given: You draw:

1. Show more of the right wall.

2. Show more of the ceiling.

3. Show more of the floor.

INDEX